Mammoth Meat

LOVE UNVEILED: HOW CAVEMAN GENETICS SHAPE MODERN RELATIONSHIPS

Douglas B Sims, PhD

Mammoth Meat

Douglas B Sims

Mammoth Meat

Table of Contents

Acknowledgments vi

Forward vii

1. Unearthing Your Inner Caveman: Ancient Wisdom for Today's Chaos 1

2. Caveman Love: Clubbing Through Today's Dating Scene 13

3. Social Jungle: Cavewomen Navigating Friend Drama 24

4. Bro Bonds: From Grunts to Genuine Bromance.....................58

5. Love in Mammoth Times: Caveman and Cavewoman Romance Tips...76

6. Caveman Communication: Grunt Decoding 101 83

7. Desire Decoded: Caveman 'Zug Zug' Insights 97

8. From Cave Paintings to Hormones: The Truth About 'Zug Zug' 101

9. The Sensitive Caveman: A Deep Dive into Feelings 110

10. Mammoth Hunt: Surviving Long-Term Love...................... 115

11. Cave Art to Romance: Passion in the Stone Age.................. 120

12. Grunts to Greatness: Caveman Chat Skills........................... 125

13. Mammoth Miscommunications: Talk Like a Caveman 140

14. Gender Roles: From Mammoths to Modernity 149

15. Grunts to Conversations: Relationship Secrets Unlocked..... 157

16. Love Through the Ages: From Fire to Tinder 160

Caveman Chronicles: The Sources................................. 163

Acknowledgments

I would like to express my deepest gratitude to my wife for her unwavering support, guidance, and the incredible journey of love and marriage we have shared for over 34 years. Your presence has been my anchor and inspiration throughout life and this process.

I am also profoundly grateful to our two children, who have enriched our lives and taught us the joys and challenges of parenting. Your growth and experiences have been a constant source of pride and learning.

To our family: Thank you for being part of our journey and for your unwavering support along the way. Your companionship and encouragement have been invaluable.

I extend my heartfelt thanks to my friends and colleagues. Observing your lives, receiving your input, and sharing insights with you have greatly contributed to this book. Your contributions have been wonderful and indispensable, and I am grateful for your role in this endeavor. Sharing our lives with you and having you share your lives with us added depth and real-world perspectives to this work. Your openness and experience have been invaluable.

Lastly, I acknowledge the countless individuals observed in local malls, theaters, and across the world. Your everyday interactions and behaviors have provided equally valuable insights and enriched the content and understanding within these pages. Thank you all for being part of this journey.

Forward

Amidst the tranquil setting of Kailua-Kona, Hawaii, two professionals—a beer-sipping anthropologist and a steak-chomping geochemist—delved into the complexities of human behavior, love, marriage, and why we do what we do as couples. With a few beers (vincha) and mammoth-sized steaks (ool) fueling their discussion, they viewed modern relationships through the lens of our caveman and cavewoman ancestors. They marveled at how despite technological advancements and changing societal norms, the core motivations for companionship, emotional connection, and intimacy have stayed as rock-solid as a Flintstones rerun.

Their conversation highlighted the resilience of these fundamental social needs, unaffected by the march of time and tech. They explored how courtship rituals like flirting and bonding have evolved while still playing a crucial role in building relationships.

Cultural norms, they found, reveal universal themes of attraction, compatibility, and commitment, transcending historical eras and geographical boundaries. Even as they acknowledged the reshaping of dating methods by technology, they emphasized that the timeless quest for connection and intimacy persists, just with fewer grunts and more swipes.

The duo's discussion also touched on the broader implications for contemporary relationship dynamics, noting that mate selection remains rooted in evolutionary imperatives from our days of living in a cave. Whether it's for long-term companionship or reproduction, these age-old behaviors continue to shape dating practices across cultures. They also pondered whether modern dating mirrors the experiences of our prehistoric ancestors, concluding that while the methods may have changed, the motivations—financial stability, emotional compatibility, shared values, and mutual respect—remain fundamentally the same.

Chapter 1

Unearthing Your Inner Caveman: Ancient Wisdom for Today's Chaos

Books like *Men Are from Mars, Women Are from Venus, Why Do Men Have Nipples, The 5 Love Languages: The Secret to Love that Last,* and many others humorously explore the fascinating differences between the sexes, delving into biological, psychological, and sociocultural factors that shape our behaviors and interactions. They blend scientific insights with lighthearted anecdotes, making complex topics accessible and engaging, by examining communication styles, emotional responses, and quirky curiosities about the human body. These books aim to bridge the gap between men and women, fostering better understanding and empathy. However, they often overlook the evolutionary perspective, neglecting to explain how these factors stem from our caveman and cavewoman genetics.

This book dives into modern relationships with a humorous prehistoric twist, uncovering why we do what we do in the realms of dating, marriage, and family. Imagine this: what did a caveman look for in a cavewoman 12,000 years ago? Well, a caveman wanted a cavewoman who could gather berries, nurture the young, and be the ultimate prehistoric support system—basically, the cave-era version of a multitasking queen. On the flip side, a cavewoman was on the lookout for a caveman who could bring home the Mammoth Meat, flex those muscles, make them laugh when times are hard, and protect the family from apex predators.

Fast forward to today, and the Mammoth Meat has transformed into the almighty US dollar and sports cars for the modern caveman. Meanwhile, gathering now means collecting purses, shoes, clothes, and all the essentials for the modern cavewoman. Nothing has really changed in 12,000 years except what we're collecting, hunting, and flashing. It's the ultimate stone-age love story, filled with laughs and timeless truths!

Okay, here we go into the ritualized world of modern dating. Today, dating is a complex dance of attraction and compatibility, reflecting our primal instincts as we seek mates for both emotional connection and survival; driven by ancient factors while navigating modern digital landscapes and social rituals, much like our caveman ancestors did through fire-lit gatherings and communal hunts. This book will describe these dynamics for the modern caveman and cavewoman, helping modern people better understand their dating patterns and find success in the contemporary romantic wilderness. Moreover, this book covers all relationships from LGBTQ+ to those old-fashioned man-woman duos (remember them?), it covers everyone.

Dating today is like time-traveling back to the Stone Age but with smartphones and slightly fancier caves. Whether you're swiping right or gifting mammoth tusks, the essence remains unchanged: humans trying to figure out love, one awkward date at a time. This book isn't just about ancient mating rituals; it's a crash course in understanding why we do the things we do in love. We've woven insights from professional papers and books into our narrative, framing them as interactions with cavemen and cavewomen to make this book both fun and enjoyable to read. Whether you're chasing bison or swiping on Grindr, deep down, we're all just looking for that special someone who gets our cave paintings.

Throughout history, humans have been relentlessly seeking Netflix-and-chill partners, proving that some things never change—whether it's Stone Age cave dwellers or Silicon Valley techies. In the modern world, we do much of the same courting as our ancient brothers and sisters did, though with modern tools and words. In the ancient caves of romance, men were like mammoth-chasing superheroes, flexing their muscles and showing off their mammoth-slaying skills to woo their cave girls. They brought home the biggest tusks and flashed their best cave paintings to prove they weren't just any old cave dude—they were the ultimate providers.

Meanwhile, cave girls weren't just sitting pretty by the fire, waiting for the biggest mammoth to be dragged home. They were eyeing the cave dudes who could draw the best mammoth murals and tell the most thrilling tales of mammoth hunts. They wanted a caveman to protect them from saber-toothed tigers and warm their cave with stories and sturdy mammoth fur. Together, these ancient lovebirds navigated the treacherous terrain of mammoth-sized challenges and cave intrigue. It was a prehistoric dance of mammoth feasting, cave-painting prowess, and finding that perfect cave partner who could balance mammoth hunting with heartfelt mammoth cuddles.

From flirting to awkward small talk, dating has evolved like a Kardashian wardrobe, but at its core, it's still about finding someone to share your snacks with. Whether you're swapping seashells or emojis, the pursuit of companionship remains as timeless as deciphering hieroglyphic love notes. Whether you're wooing with flowers or memes, remember: behind every swipe, a human is looking for a love connection and maybe a good laugh along the way.

Navigating Modern Love: A Caveman's Perspective

Modern dating rituals have evolved significantly from our cave-dwelling ancestors, yet they still retain elements of showcasing abilities, demonstrating compatibility, and building connections. In the digital age, men often start by crafting an appealing online presence, curating social media profiles, and participating in online dating apps to showcase their interests, hobbies, and lifestyle. Think of it as the modern equivalent of painting a mastodon hunt on the cave wall, except with fewer spears and more selfies.

Men typically take the initiative in making the first move through online messaging, texting, or approaching someone in person. This delicate dance involves balancing confidence and respect, aiming to spark interest without appearing too forward—essentially, the 21st-century version of grunting impressively by the fire. When planning dates, men strive to impress by choosing interesting and thoughtful venues. From trendy restaurants and unique bars to adventurous outings and cultural events, this reflects their creativity and effort. Imagine planning a night out that says, "I can hunt and gather the best sushi in town." Modern men also emphasize their stability and potential as partners by highlighting their career achievements, financial stability, and future aspirations. It's like waving a big, metaphorical spear that says, "I can provide and protect... and also, I have a 401k."

Women, on the other hand, craft their online presence carefully, using social media and dating apps to present their best selves. They evaluate potential partners based on profiles, looking for signs of compatibility, shared interests, and mutual values. It's like swiping through a digital forest, searching for the perfect mate who also enjoys hiking and has a golden retriever. Typically, women engage in conversations initiated by men, using these interactions to assess personality traits, humor, and communication skills. They look for red flags and green lights, gauging the potential for a meaningful connection—think of it as an advanced form of gathering berries but with a lot more ghosting involved. While men often plan initial dates, women contribute by suggesting subsequent venues and activities. This collaborative approach ensures mutual enjoyment and reflects their preferences and interests. It's like saying, "Sure, I enjoyed the mammoth hunt, but how about we try berry-picking next time?"

Modern women emphasize their independence and personal achievements, including career success, hobbies, and social circles. They showcase their ability to lead fulfilling lives on their own while being open to a partnership. It's the contemporary equivalent of showing off a perfectly organized cave and a thriving herb garden. Couples engage in a variety of shared experiences, from dining out and attending events to traveling and trying new activities. These experiences help them bond and discover shared interests and values. It's like going on a mammoth hunt together, except with fewer tusks and more tapas.

Open and honest communication is crucial in modern dating. Texting, calling, and video chatting help maintain connections and build emotional intimacy, allowing both parties to express their feelings and expectations. Think of it as a never-ending drum circle where everyone tries to stay in rhythm without missing a beat. Introducing each other to friends and family is a significant step, helping gauge the acceptance and support of their relationship from loved ones. As relationships progress, discussions about future plans become important, including conversations about career goals, living arrangements, and long-term aspirations. It's like planning the layout of a new cave together, complete with where to put the fire pit and the best spots for hunting murals.

Modern dating rituals blend traditional elements of showcasing abilities and building connections with contemporary practices of digital engagement and open communication. Men often initiate and plan, highlighting their stability and creativity, while women evaluate and engage, showcasing their independence and achievements. Together, they create a dynamic dance of mutual respect, shared experiences, and future planning, navigating the complex landscape of modern relationships— proving that even after all these years, the dance of love is still the best show in the Stone Age.

Ultimately, dating around the globe is like trying different flavors of ice cream—some are spicy, some are sweet, but they all come with that universal hope of finding the one cone that won't melt on you. Whether you're navigating arranged marriages or swiping through a sea of selfies, the quest for attraction, compatibility, and commitment is as old as trying to sneak extra dessert without getting caught. Therefore, here's to love, laughter, and the occasional awkward cultural misunderstanding along the way. After all, no matter where you are, everyone deserves a shot at finding their perfect flavor of romance.

Between sips of coffee and juggling our wild kids, we've wondered: Are modern dating struggles just ancient caveman conundrums with fancier distractions? From swiping right to sharing cave lion selfies, the pursuit of connection and intimacy hasn't changed much. Sure, our tools have gone from stone axes to smartphones, but deep down, we're all still hoping to find someone who won't steal our mammoth steaks.

Let's not forget marriage—whether you're trading rocks or Netflix passwords, it's all about finding a partner to help navigate this crazy journey called life. Ancient civilizations may have bartered for land, but nowadays, it's more about sharing Wi-Fi and deciding whose turn it is to take out the trash. As we ponder why we swipe and tie the knot, one thing's for sure: whether you're a caveman or a Zoom-dating enthusiast, the quest for love is timeless—and occasionally hilarious.

Ah, the age-old mystery of dating: Men think they're jumping through hoops of fire to impress women, while women feel like they're dodging those fiery hoops while holding a bouquet of expectations. It's a dance as old as time, where everyone's trying to bring their A-game without tripping over their shoelaces. And let's talk money—because in the game of love, financial stability can be the difference between Netflix and chill or Netflix and bills. Whether you're balancing the checkbook or swiping right on a six-figure salary, let's face it: love might be blind, but it sure has 20/20 vision when it comes to bank account balances.

Marriage? Oh, that ancient ritual that once secured land and societal status. Nowadays, it's more about securing a joint bank account (the new mammoth meat) and a shared Netflix password. Because who needs a dowry when you've got Amazon Prime delivering everything you need right to your doorstep?

In the end, whether you're navigating the complexities of dating or planning your financial future, just remember that love may not cost a thing, but it sure doesn't hurt to have a good credit score.

The Caveman's and Cavewomen's Guide to Attraction

Influenced by personal preferences and cultural factors, men and women often look for the following traits in a partner:

✓ **Beauty and Personality**: Beauty is in the eye of the beholder and while looks are fleeting, a killer personality is like fine wine—it matures and improves with time. So, rather than solely focusing on external appearances, nurture your inner qualities and shine from the inside out.

✓ **Snuggles and Smooches**: To inject warmth into your relationship, skip the pricey therapy sessions and opt for a heartfelt bear hug followed by a playful tickle fight—it's not only more affordable but also heaps more enjoyable.

✓ **Caring and Compassionate**: Being caring and compassionate is akin to wielding a cheat code for success. It's like having a potent love potion that genuinely works—just sprinkle in empathy, and you'll ignite sparks of genuine connection.

✓ **Exceptional Communication**: Finding someone who shares your passions and can geek out with you is often likened to discovering a pot of gold at the end of the rainbow. Exceptional communication means you never have to argue about what series to binge-watch next; instead, it's about relishing in the shared excitement and mutual interests that deepen your connection.

✓ **Family-Oriented and Nurturing**: Being caregiving and family-oriented is akin to holding the MVP title in relationship material. If you possess the ability to nurture others with expertise while also handling practical tasks like taking out the trash, you're undoubtedly a catch.

✓ **Supportive**: Supporting your partner's dreams isn't merely a nice gesture—it's akin to pouring rocket fuel into your relationship's engine. When you actively fuel their aspirations, you're propelling your love to new heights and witnessing it soar.

✓ **Trustworthy**: Trustworthiness serves as the superhero cape of relationships—wear it with pride! When you're known for your reliability and honesty, you become the Clark Kent of love: unassuming on the surface but a true superhero within.

✓ **Emotionally Stable**: Emotional regulation is a powerful skill that sets relationship champions apart. Maintaining your composure during challenging times is like possessing a superpower. By staying calm and collected, you demonstrate resilience and maturity that can navigate any storm.

✓ **Shared Values**: Shared values are the jackpot of love, akin to winning the lottery. When you find someone who shares your quirks and dreams, it's like discovering a rare gem. Compatibility becomes crucial because those playful arguments over who gets the last slice of pizza or the remote are signs of genuine connection and shared experiences.

In the quest for a fulfilling relationship, nurturing inner beauty and personality is paramount, as external appearances are fleeting. Embracing the essence of who we are from within our personalities, like a fine wine, mature and improve with time. Infusing warmth into your relationship doesn't require expensive therapy; simple, heartfelt gestures like bear hugs and playful tickle fights create joy and strengthen bonds. Being caring and compassionate acts as a powerful love potion, where empathy sparks genuine connections. Exceptional communication transforms shared interests into golden moments, eliminating trivial arguments and deepening mutual excitement. A family-oriented and nurturing partner is a true MVP, balancing practical tasks with the ability to care deeply for others. Supporting your partner's dreams is akin to pouring rocket fuel into the relationship, propelling it to new heights. Trustworthiness, the superhero cape of relationships, underpins reliability and honesty, making you a true hero in love. Emotional stability, a superpower in itself, showcases resilience and maturity, guiding relationships through any storm. Lastly, shared values are the ultimate jackpot, bringing compatibility to the forefront and turning simple moments into rare gems of connection. By cultivating these qualities, you unlock the secrets to enduring love and happiness.

In the intricate dance of attraction and compatibility, emotional intelligence might just be more valuable than your IQ score. Whether you're trading mammoth meat or swiping credit cards, finding that perfect partner boils down to mutual respect, shared values, and the ability to laugh at each other's terrible jokes. By focusing on these core elements, you lay the foundation for a relationship that is not only enduring but also deeply fulfilling, proving that true connection transcends time and societal changes.

Modern Men and Women: The New Hunters and Gatherers

Modern men are more like prehistoric hunters but with fancier tools and better grooming. Imagine a caveman, spear in hand, chasing a mammoth. Now replace the spear with a smartphone and the mammoth with a promotion, and you've got the modern man. With the same level of determination, they hunt for career success, financial stability, and personal achievements as if their next meal depended on it. Just as prehistoric hunters faced off against wild beasts, modern men take on the perils of office politics, extreme sports, and DIY home improvement projects, showing their fearless nature (or sheer stubbornness).

Modern men flaunt their alpha prowess in today's urban landscape with the skill of a caveman who just discovered the wheel. Instead of chasing and killing a mammoth, they conquer the modern jungle with career promotions with prestigious job titles, striding through office corridors as if they've tamed corporate beasts akin to cave bears. Their financial acumen becomes their battle axe, wielding sleek cars, robust investment portfolios, and homes that proclaim success. They stay fit by going to the gym, running marathons, and mastering cutting-edge gadgets to become the tech wizards of their tribe. Leadership shines through team management and social finesse, whether hosting legendary barbecues or networking like seasoned pros.

Personal style serves as their contemporary plumage, flaunting impeccably tailored suits and groomed appearances that exude confidence and authority. From fixing household mishaps to navigating business challenges, their resourcefulness and problem-solving skills rival any ancient survival tactic. Their adventurous spirit thrives in extreme sports and entrepreneurial endeavors, showcasing their alpha status among other men with modern flair, more Wi-Fi connectivity, and significantly less mud.

Modern women are like prehistoric gatherers, but instead of foraging for berries, they're juggling careers, family, social lives, and self-care with the finesse of a circus performer. Picture a gatherer with a basket full of roots and herbs; now picture a modern woman with a smartphone, a yoga mat, and a conference call in progress. Their multitasking prowess is legendary, much like their ancient counterparts who balanced the needs of their communities.

Back in the day, gatherers had to know which plants were edible and which ones would make you see colors that didn't exist. Today, women navigate the equally treacherous landscapes of office politics, social networks, shopping malls and online shopping sales. Their ability to find the best deals, solve problems, and adapt to the ever-changing world is like spotting a ripe berry patch amid a thorny bush.

Prehistoric gatherers were the original social networkers, maintaining community bonds and passing down essential knowledge. Modern women are the glue that holds families and communities together, organizing birthday parties, sharing life hacks, and ensuring everyone's emotional well-being. They're the ones who remember your birthday, your dog's name, and how you like your coffee —all while managing a spreadsheet and a toddler.

The nurturing essence of ancient gatherers thrives in modern women, who excel in providing compassionate care and support in various roles. Like their predecessors who ensured the sustenance and well-being of their communities through gathering and caregiving, contemporary women exhibit unparalleled capabilities in nurturing others. Whether comforting a distraught child, mentoring colleagues in the workplace, or leading initiatives that benefit their communities, their nurturing instincts shine through. While the setting has evolved from caves to comfortable homes and from communal fires to slow cookers, the core essence of providing emotional and practical support remains unchanged.

These lighthearted comparisons highlight modern women's remarkable adaptability, resourcefulness, and community-mindedness. In navigating a world that presents increasingly complex challenges, women adeptly assume multiple roles as multitaskers, nurturers, and problem-solvers. They embody the legacy of their prehistoric ancestors who thrived by adapting to environmental changes and collaborating for collective well-being. Today, women continue to embody these traits, seamlessly balancing diverse responsibilities and overcoming obstacles with creativity and determination.

Alpha Caveman Meets Alpha Cavewoman: A Love Story with a Twist

Picture this: an Alpha caveman and an Alpha cavewoman walk into a relationship. Sounds like the start of a joke, right? Well, buckle up, because it's a wild ride. With their strong personalities and leadership vibes, it's like watching two captains trying to steer the same ship—cue the power struggles and epic battles for control of the tribe. These two aren't just making suggestions; they're issuing commands. Compromise? More like a foreign language. Collaboration? Only if it means they both get to be in charge.

In the daily lives of early humans, every decision was a potential battleground—a contest of wills from choosing the best spot for the evening fire to determining who deserved the prime cut of mammoth meat. These moments were less about cooperative problem-solving and more about asserting dominance and proving superiority. Imagine them locked in a standoff, standing defiantly with arms crossed, each unwilling to yield—an atmosphere where collaboration took a back seat to individual prowess and competition for status.

Their competitive streaks added fuel to the fire, turning everyday decisions into never-ending matches reminiscent of two cave people locked in perpetual conflict. Neither was willing to concede, transforming their relationship into a constant struggle for dominance. Disagreements escalated into epic debates, with each party using wit and determination to assert their viewpoint. Even mundane tasks like berry picking or hunting became opportunities to showcase skill and outperform the other, whether by finding the largest berries or bringing down the most impressive game.

Despite the ongoing tug-of-war, an undeniable spark ignited between them. Their mutual respect for each other's strength and determination fueled an intense connection, albeit one marked by turbulence. While they clashed over minor issues, the passion underlying each confrontation was palpable. It created a dynamic where respect and rivalry coexisted, making their relationship simultaneously exhilarating and exhausting. In this complex interplay of competition and admiration, they found themselves drawn to each other's fierce spirit, forging a bond that thrived on the thrill of challenge and the satisfaction of overcoming obstacles together.

Who would have thought that love could resemble such an extreme sport? In the fiery dynamic between two strong-willed Alphas, sparks fly more often than tranquil moments are shared. Yet, there's an undeniable magnetism in their passionate bond. Their relationship challenges conventional notions of love, demonstrating that intense partnerships can thrive amidst competition and conflict. It's a union that redefines the essence of love itself, illustrating that sometimes, the deepest connections are forged in the crucible of challenge and rivalry. Despite the tumultuous nature of their interactions, their bond remains compelling, showcasing the resilience and depth that can emerge when two fiercely independent spirits come together.

The Timeless Quest for Love

In the end, whether you're hunting mammoths or hunting for a modern match online, the quest for love remains timeless. Our tools may have evolved from stone axes to smartphones, but the essence of romance is as ancient as the caves our ancestors painted. Through awkward dates, heartfelt gestures, and the pursuit of that special connection, we're all just modern-day cave dwellers trying to navigate the complexities of human relationships. This book has journeyed through the ages, blending humor and insight to shed light on the timeless dance of love. Therefore, whether you're swiping, texting, or sharing mammoth steaks, remember: deep down, we're all just looking for someone who understands our cave paintings and makes the journey worthwhile.

Chapter 2

Caveman Love: Clubbing Through Today's Dating Scene

E ver wondered why navigating the dating scene feels akin to solving a Rubik's Cube blindfolded? This book serves as your ultimate guide, offering a cheat code to unravel the mysteries of love in today's chaotic world. Think of it as a GPS for your heart, skillfully guiding you through the intricate jungle of modern relationships while teaching invaluable lessons in patience as you seek out "the One"—because, unfortunately, they don't come with a convenient Google Maps pin.

This book equips us with essential tools to enhance our relationships and marriages, emphasizing the importance of patience in the quest for true love. It delves into the underlying motivations that drive our search for that special person. Today, just as our ancestors did 100,000 years ago, men and women still yearn for fundamental needs like sustenance, shelter, and a partner who won't monopolize the mammoth steak. However, modern challenges have added new criteria to the mix, such as Wi-Fi reliability and compatibility for binge-watching on Netflix, shaping contemporary relationship expectations.

Attraction is a scientific rollercoaster journey that spans from the basics of biology to the intricate choreography of emotional connection, a ride fascinating enough to even pique the interest of Charles Darwin himself.

This dynamic voyage delves into the primal instincts hardwired into our DNA, illuminating how the drive for survival and reproduction has shaped our preferences and behaviors. It explores the neurological fireworks that ignite when we encounter someone who ticks all the right boxes, dissecting the roles of dopamine, oxytocin, and other chemicals in fostering connection and attachment.

But the ride doesn't stop at biology. It also navigates through the complex landscape of psychological factors, where early childhood experiences, personal insecurities, and subconscious desires play pivotal roles. The journey reveals how social conditioning and cultural narratives influence our perceptions of attractiveness and compatibility, guiding our choices in the modern dating world.

Buckle up for this enlightening ride, as understanding the motivations behind why Caveman and Cavewoman swipe right or left could hold the key to unlocking your own romantic evolution. By examining the dance between nature and nurture, you'll gain insights into the mysterious forces driving your attraction patterns and relationship dynamics. This knowledge not only enhances self-awareness but also equips you with the tools to navigate the dating scene with confidence and clarity, ensuring your quest for companionship is as successful as it is fulfilling. So, get ready to decode the science of attraction and embark on a transformative journey toward   finding and fostering meaningful connections.

Shake It Up: The Vital Role of Dancing in Courtship

Dancing isn't just about moves—it's a confident statement of style and a playful invitation to connect through rhythm, laughter, and shared moments on the dance floor. Dancing is a time-honored tradition where men and women alike compete not only for attention but for a deeper connection, moving to the rhythm of courtship.

For Cavewomen

Women hit the dance floor in the dating scene for a medley of reasons that could rival a DJ's playlist. Firstly, dancing isn't just about showing off moves; it's a statement of confidence and flair. It's like saying, "Hey, look at me—I can drop it like it's hot and still keep my cool." Secondly, it's the ultimate social icebreaker. Nothing says "Let's groove together" quite like synchronized body shimmies and a shared awkward laugh when someone steps on your toes. Plus, let's not forget the ancient art of non-verbal communication through dance moves. It's like a secret code of winks, spins, and hip sways that says, "I'm interested, and I've got rhythm." Culturally, dancing might seem like just steps and beats, but it's also a nod to traditions and a way to fit in—or stand out—in the dating game. Ultimately, whether it's salsa, hip-hop, or a spontaneous kitchen dance-off, women know that when the music starts, the fun begins, and who knows? That next dance partner might just be a step away from becoming something more.

For Cavemen

Dancing plays a pivotal role in courtship dynamics for men by providing a unique avenue for self-expression and communication. Through dance, men can convey confidence, rhythm, and creativity, all of which are qualities often admired in potential partners. Physically, dancing enhances coordination, agility, and stamina, contributing to overall fitness and vitality, which can further enhance attractiveness. Despite these benefits, some men may hesitate to dance due to various factors such as social anxiety, fear of judgment, or cultural perceptions about masculinity and dancing. These barriers can limit their willingness to engage in this form of expression despite its potential social and personal benefits. Breaking down these barriers involves fostering inclusive environments that celebrate the joy, physical benefits, and social connections that dancing offers. By encouraging men to embrace dancing as a positive and enjoyable activity, we can promote greater confidence, social engagement, and relationship-building skills through this universal form of human expression.

The Chemistry of Sexual Attraction

Ultimately, sexual attraction between men and women, or Caveman and Cavewoman, emerges from a complex interplay of biological, psychological, and social factors, each layer contributing to the intricate mosaic of human relationships. Biologically, the foundation of attraction is laid by evolutionary imperatives. Men and women are subconsciously driven to seek out traits that signify fertility, health, and genetic robustness. These primal instincts, honed over millennia, ensure the continuation of the species by promoting the selection of partners who exhibit signs of vitality and reproductive capability. This is why physical attributes such as facial symmetry, body shape, and even pheromones play a significant role in initial attraction.

Psychologically, individual experiences and personality traits add another layer of complexity to attraction. Our early childhood interactions, attachment styles, and past relationships shape our preferences and influence how we connect with others. For instance, someone who experienced nurturing and secure relationships in their formative years might seek out similar traits in their partners, gravitating towards those who exude warmth and reliability. Conversely, unresolved traumas or negative experiences can lead individuals to subconsciously repeat unhealthy patterns or seek out partners who fulfill certain psychological needs, whether positive or negative.

Social factors further enrich the tapestry of attraction. Cultural norms, societal expectations, and media portrayals shape our perceptions of what is desirable or acceptable in a partner. These influences can vary widely across different societies and historical periods, illustrating how malleable and context-dependent human attraction can be. For instance, in some cultures, financial stability and social status may be highly valued traits, while in others, intellectual prowess or artistic talent might be more highly esteemed. Social dynamics also play out in the way we engage in courtship rituals, from the grandiose displays of wealth or strength seen in historical and tribal societies to the nuanced, often digital flirtations of the modern age.

At the heart of this intricate dance lies the innate human desire for intimacy, connection, and companionship. Despite the layers of complexity added by biology, psychology, and society, the fundamental need to bond with another person remains constant. This drive for connection is not merely about reproduction; it encompasses the profound emotional and psychological fulfillment that comes from being understood, valued, and loved by another.

These dynamics have evolved over millennia yet remain fundamentally rooted in our shared human experience. From the prehistoric caves where our ancestors first painted their stories on stone walls to the virtual spaces where we now share our lives, the essence of human attraction endures. It is a testament to our resilience and adaptability, reflecting how we have navigated and continue to navigate the ever-changing landscapes of love and relationships.

In understanding this complex interplay, we gain valuable insights into ourselves and our interactions with others. We learn to appreciate the depth and richness of our emotional lives and recognize the profound continuity that links us with all of humanity across time. By embracing the complexity of attraction, we not only enhance our own relationships but also contribute to the ongoing narrative of human connection that has been unfolding for countless generations.

Biological Instincts

Ever wondered why cavemen and cavewomen were so enthusiastic about "zug zug"? It all boils down to the primal urge for the survival of the species—a quest to ensure that their clan's genetic legacy endured longer than even the mighty woolly mammoth. In the rugged landscape of early human societies, reproduction wasn't just about personal gratification; it was a strategic move to propagate traits and skills vital for the group's survival. This drive to reproduce wasn't merely instinctual but a calculated effort to strengthen familial ties and secure the future by passing down advantageous genetic material. Thus, "zug zug" wasn't just about fulfilling immediate desires but laying the foundation for the continued prosperity and resilience of their lineage in a challenging and unpredictable environment.

Physical Attraction

In the Stone Age dating arena, physical appearance held significant sway—attributes signaling health and fertility were more alluring than a perfectly roasted cave bear steak! Much like selecting the finest flint for crafting spears, the choice of a mate was crucial. A robust physique and vibrant appearance indicated not only immediate attractiveness but also the potential to contribute robust offspring to the tribe's survival. In this primal setting, the stakes were high, with each selection carrying implications for the future resilience and prosperity of the group. Thus, "looks" weren't merely superficial; they were a practical consideration in ensuring the continuation and vitality of the community's lineage amidst the challenges of their environment.

Chemical Factors

Hormones such as testosterone and estrogen acted as potent love potions in the Stone Age, igniting passions and intensifying connections with primal fervor. Like alchemical forces, these biological agents played a pivotal role in shaping romantic dynamics, causing hearts to race and igniting fires of desire. Testosterone, associated with vitality and assertiveness, fueled the pursuit of mates and dominance within social hierarchies, while estrogen, with its nurturing and empathetic qualities, enhanced emotional bonds and contributed to reproductive readiness. In the ancient realm of human interaction, these hormonal influences weren't just physiological; they were catalysts for profound emotional and social interactions, shaping the very fabric of early human relationships and ensuring the continuation of the species in a challenging world. Thus, "caveman chemistry" epitomized the intricate dance of attraction and reproduction, where hormonal signals orchestrated the primal symphony of love and survival.

Emotional Connection

Getting cozy by the fire in ancient times held a significance beyond mere warmth—it symbolized the forging of bonds as strong as the walls of a cave bear's den. In the flickering light of the flames, sharing that intimate space meant more than just physical proximity; it signified a deep level of trust and emotional connection. It was a moment of vulnerability and companionship, where individuals entrusted each other with their safety, comfort, and perhaps even their dreams for the future. Sharing that closeness wasn't merely about sharing the last bite of a roasted root or the warmth of the fire; it was about sharing hopes, fears, and aspirations—the very essence of what it means to build a lasting relationship based on mutual understanding and support. Thus, by the firelight, bonds were woven that transcended the immediate need for warmth, weaving a tapestry of trust and intimacy that strengthened the fabric of early human communities.

Pleasure and Satisfaction

If "zug zug" didn't bring joy, cavemen wouldn't have pursued it with such fervor! It's akin to the exhilaration of discovering fire for the first time—a primal experience that not only feels inherently satisfying but also becomes a cornerstone of daily life. Much like the warmth and comfort of a roaring fire, "zug zug" provided a sense of fulfillment and connection that was essential for the well-being of early human communities. It wasn't just about physical pleasure; it represented a fundamental aspect of human existence—a bond that strengthened social ties and ensured the continuation of the clan. The allure of "zug zug" wasn't merely in the act itself but in its ability to foster intimacy, trust, and unity among individuals, laying the groundwork for cooperation and shared purpose. In this way, "zug zug" mirrored the discovery of fire: a discovery that felt good and kept humanity coming back for more, shaping the course of human evolution and social interaction.

Communication and Intimacy

"Zug zug" transcended mere physicality—it was a profound form of communication and connection among early humans. More than just grunt and groan, it was the original heart-to-heart talk, where emotions, desires, and vulnerabilities were laid bare. In the flickering light of the cave, sharing that intimate connection was akin to painting the walls with feelings, creating a tapestry of shared experiences and deepening bonds. It was a language of touch and closeness that conveyed understanding and affection, fostering trust and solidarity within the clan. Through "zug zug", individuals expressed their deepest yearnings and fears, forging relationships that were not only physical but also emotional and spiritual.

It was a sacred act that affirmed belonging and strengthened social cohesion, ensuring the continuity and resilience of early human communities. Thus, "zug zug" wasn't just a primal instinct—it was a profound expression of humanity's need for connection and intimacy, etching its significance into the very fabric of human relationships and societal development.

Social and Cultural Influences: Keeping Up with the Neanderthals

In the Stone Age, societal norms and expectations played a crucial role in shaping the dynamics of relationships and intimacy. Sexual activity, or "zug zug", wasn't just a spontaneous act but adhered to certain rules and conventions that governed who initiated and how they pursued their desires. Like a dance choreographed by ancient customs, even cavemen had their own set of guidelines dictating who chased whom through the bushes.

Pairing up wasn't just about finding a soulmate; it was about ensuring your offspring didn't become lunch for a wolf. It's like the original "swipe right to survive" scenario, where compatibility meant not getting eaten and having enough rocks to build a decent fire pit. Next time you complain about modern dating, keep in mind, at least you're not trying to impress someone with your ability to make fire from scratch. Thank your lucky stars for takeout and indoor plumbing, because dating used to be a lot hairier—literally and figuratively!

Reproductive Instincts: Baby Fever and Other Quirks

Back in ancient times, cavemen and cavewomen were primarily focused on ensuring the continuity of their lineage—the survival and propagation of their family tree. It was akin to striving to ensure that their family tree had more branches than a tangled vine in a dense jungle. This primal drive wasn't just about personal fulfillment but about securing the future of their clan and community.

Physical Attraction: The Magnetism Mystery
In the Stone Age dating scene, appearances were not merely about aesthetics but essential for survival and reproduction. Men showcased their physical prowess as if they were preparing for a mammoth wrestling match, their muscles bulging, and bodies honed through hunting and physical labor. This display wasn't just for show; it signaled strength, endurance, and the ability to provide and protect—a crucial factor in attracting a mate and ensuring the survival of offspring.

Social Bonds and Group Cohesion: The Friendship Glue
Pairing up in the Stone Age wasn't solely about romantic attraction; it was integral to fostering social bonds and enhancing group cohesion, essential for survival and success. Whether hunting mammoths or wrangling wild boars, forming relationships allowed cavemen and cavewomen to collaborate effectively, functioning as a cohesive unit like super glue in the face of challenges.

Prehistoric Teamwork: Men Lifted, Women Led—Yabba Dabba Do!
In the rugged landscape of the Stone Age, survival often depended on a division of labor that played to each gender's strengths. Men took on physically demanding tasks like hunting mammoths and defending the group against predators, showcasing their strength and skill as providers and protectors. Meanwhile, women assumed pivotal roles in managing daily life and nurturing familial bonds. They oversaw tasks such as gathering berries, tending to children, and maintaining the communal hearth—a crucial hub for warmth, cooking, and social interaction.

The Love Glue: Sticking Together with Feels
Back in the day, emotions in early human societies were like the original reality TV drama series—trust and affection were the key plot twists that kept everyone hooked! Trust among cavemen and cavewomen wasn't just about who could be relied upon not to eat all the berries—it was a prehistoric pact thicker than mammoth fur! Affection in early human tribes wasn't just about cozy cave cuddles—it was a full-contact sport!

Establishing emotional connections in the Stone Age wasn't just about finding your cave soulmate—it was like speed dating with spears and grunts! For early humans, trust was the foundation upon which communal life was built. It facilitated cooperation in hunting, gathering, and defending against external threats. Affection and emotional support nurtured a sense of security and belonging within the community, fostering resilience and unity in the face of adversity.

The Evolution of Love and Survival

Ah, the epic saga of Cavemen and Cavewomen of over 12,000 years: the original odd couple who discovered that love and survival go together like rocks and a hard place. When they weren't arguing over whose turn it was to hunt or gather, they were busy inventing the first-ever cave chore chart. But let's give credit where it's due—despite their differences (like who gets the bigger cave corner), they figured out that teamwork makes the dream work. Sure, their idea of a romantic dinner was probably roasted dinosaur ribs, but hey, it kept the sparks alive!

And then came climate change—talk about a plot twist! Suddenly, they had to innovate or freeze their loincloths off. From agriculture to the wheel, they were like the MacGyvers of survival, proving that sometimes adversity makes you invent stuff (and maybe argue less about whose turn it is to clean the cave or wash the dishes).

But let's not forget the real challenge: understanding each other. Men wanted to talk about mammoth-hunting strategies, while women were more into cave décor and fire safety protocols. It's like trying to explain TikTok to a saber-toothed tiger—sure, you might end up with fewer misunderstandings if you just embrace the differences and laugh about it over a cave-side BBQ. Because at the end of the day, whether you're a Caveman or a Cavewoman, finding common ground (and maybe a few less cave paintings of hunting victories) is what keeps the romance alive.

Embracing Ancient Wisdom in Modern Love

Back in the day, climate change, starting 12,000 years ago, wasn't just about melting icebergs; it was like nature's original relationship counselor! As humans evolved, so did our knack for problem-solving and agriculture. But let's face it, sometimes it feels like men (the Caveman) and women (the Cavewoman) are still debating whether to handle issues with a club or a heartfelt chat by the fire. Maybe if we embrace our inner 'caveman' and 'cavewoman' wisdom, we can finally settle who gets the last slice of mammoth pizza without triggering an ice age meltdown in the kitchen!

Finally, navigating the dating scene can feel like solving a Rubik's Cube blindfolded, but with the insights from this chapter, you've now got the cheat codes to unravel the mysteries of love in today's chaotic world. Equipped with essential tools for enhancing relationships and marriages, you can approach the quest for true love with patience and understanding. Just as our ancestors yearned for sustenance, shelter, and a partner who wouldn't monopolize the mammoth steak, modern relationships require balancing old instincts with new challenges—like Wi-Fi reliability and Netflix compatibility. Remember, love is a complex blend of biology, psychology, and social factors, but with mutual respect, shared values, and a good sense of humor, you'll be well on your way to a fulfilling partnership. Whether you're swiping right or sharing mammoth steaks, the journey of love is timeless, and with a little patience, it's bound to be rewarding.

Chapter 3

Social Jungle: Cavewomen Navigating Friend Drama

U nderstanding the intricacies of female friendships is a challenging endeavor that requires both respect and a willingness to learn. As a married man with a wife, a daughter, and female friends, I don't profess to fully understand the social dynamics of female friendships or circles. It looks more intimidating than walking through a cave filled with poisonous snakes. These relationships are complex and filled with nuances, shaped by various social, emotional, and cultural factors that often differ from those observed in male friendships. I approach these dynamics with respect and a willingness to learn, acknowledging the unique experiences and perspectives that women bring to their social interactions.

Ever wonder why Cavemen brave blizzards to grill meat, and why Cavewomen have a sixth sense for shoe sales? It's like we're stuck in the Stone Age, just with upgraded fashion priorities! Seeing a friend share pictures of their middle school-aged daughter and son starting school on Facebook made me reflect on female friendships for women, young and old. As a parent, I know how tough it can be for young women to navigate friendships, having watched my daughter figure out who she is amongst other young women in public school and life after university.

I met my wife when I was 19 and she was 18 and watching her navigate the world of female politics has shown me what a different world it is compared to men. Women's friendships can feel like a covert club where the password changes faster than a chameleon on caffeine, and the initiation requires a mutual obsession with chocolate and wine.

Reflecting on female friendships has been occupying my thoughts for some time. It's not just my kids' relationships that intrigue me, but also the dynamics of adult female friendships. These relationships seem as challenging as juggling chainsaws while tap-dancing on a tightrope! Here are some of the social interactions and challenges I see, as an outsider:

TikTok Troubles: Beating the Clock

Between dodging deadlines, wrestling with family dynamics, and navigating life's general whirlpool, penciling in brunch dates can seem as elusive as catching a unicorn on camera. It's like trying to synchronize schedules with a herd of hyperactive leprechauns—just when you think you've nailed down a time, poof! It vanishes into the mythical realm of "next weekend." Juggling calendars is like herding cats; someone's always meowing about a conflicting meeting or a surprise dental appointment. So, if you manage to lock in that coveted brunch slot, celebrate it like you've discovered the pot of gold at the end of the rainbow—unicorns optional!

Life Transitions: Moving Mayhem

Having babies? Career changes? It's like playing friendship Jenga with a troupe of sneezing clowns—just when you've expertly stacked your tower of plans, someone lets out a hearty achoo! Suddenly, your carefully balanced blocks of life decisions come crashing down faster than you can say "babies and board meetings." It's a game where the rules change as often as the weather in April, and just when you think you've mastered the art of balancing diaper duty with deadlines, someone throws in a curveball like a surprise promotion or a spontaneous round of musical chairs. Grab your hard hat and brace yourself—because in this game of live Jenga, achoos and career moves are all part of the unpredictable fun!

Priorities Schmorities: Getting on the Same Page

While some are binge-watching Netflix, others are embarking on epic quests to conquer Mount Laundry—a towering peak of socks and shirts that rivals Everest in its daunting stature. Navigating this labyrinthine household adventure is like trying to decode an ancient treasure map written in detergent hieroglyphics. Just when you think you've discovered a shared interest in an action-packed series, someone shouts from the laundry room about the missing sock saga. It's a journey where unearthing common ground feels as rare as stumbling upon buried pirate gold in the backyard sandbox. Whether you're deep-diving into plot twists or unraveling the mysteries of fabric softeners, remember that in the kingdom of domestic quests, every episode watched, and every load folded is a heroic feat worthy of celebration—just maybe with less dramatic music and more applause from the peanut gallery!

Talking Tango: Mastering Communication Styles

From decoding emojis that seem to have more layers than an onion to deciphering passive-aggressive Post-it notes that rival the complexity of ancient hieroglyphics, navigating conversations can sometimes feel like playing a game of 4D chess in a room full of teleporting pawns. Just when you think you've mastered the art of interpreting "LOL" versus "ROFL," someone drops a cryptic smiley face that leaves you contemplating the meaning of life. It's a battlefield where every word spoken or typed is a strategic move, and misinterpreting a message can lead to more confusion than trying to follow IKEA assembly instructions without the Allen wrench. Grab your virtual magnifying glass and strap on your thinking cap, because in this world of digital dialogue and sticky notes, understanding the hidden meanings is the ultimate quest worthy of a heroic saga—complete with dramatic plot twists and a grand finale that involves finally figuring out who left that last passive-aggressive note about coffee cup cleanliness in the breakroom.

Trust and Vulnerability: Spill the Beans!

Navigating friendships can be as tricky as trying to hug a cactus—ouch! Each experience adds another prickly layer to the fortress of friendship Fort Knox. It's like being in the circus of life where adult female friendships are the daring high-wire act. We're all cheering them on, even though sometimes it feels like the safety net is miles away and the clowns are running amok! Regardless of whether you're tiptoeing across the tightrope of trust or juggling the complexities of shared history and inside jokes, remember that every friendship victory deserves a standing ovation—even if it comes with a few bumps and bruises along the way.

Circumnavigating these encounters is like trying to herd saber-toothed cats—patience, a good sense of humor, and maybe a well-placed bribe of mammoth jerky can go a long way. Because let's face it, in the jungle of relationships, political savvy is just as important as knowing when to share the last cave painting.

When it comes to betrayal, women might as well have a rulebook thicker than a mammoth's fur—it's like trying to decipher hieroglyphics written by someone who borrowed your favorite spear and never returned it. Whether it's squabbling over who gets the prime berry-picking spot or the last piece of mammoth jerky, the drama can rival any season of "Survivor." It's a jungle out there and navigating the treacherous waters of female friendships sometimes feels like being cast away on a remote island with a tribe of cunning contestants, each plotting their next strategic move over campfire gossip sessions. Therefore, grab your torch and watch your back, because in this wild game of social survival, trust is as scarce as a well-cooked mammoth steak—and sometimes, even harder to swallow!

But let's not paint all cave-dwellers with the same brush. Betrayal isn't just a gender thing; it's more complicated than deciding who gets the bigger chunk of mammoth meat. After all, even our ancient ancestors knew that sharing is caring—unless it's the last piece of chocolate-covered insects. Regardless of whether you're negotiating alliances or just trying to avoid being thrown under the mammoth mode of transportation, remember: a little understanding and a lot of mammoth jerky can smooth over even the rockiest of friendship cliffs.

"Women's relationships with each other are like a never-ending game of emotional tag—just when you think you've caught your breath, someone yells: Wine and Netflix break!"

The intricate maze of female friendships is akin to maneuvering through a mammoth stampede—where sharing secrets can be as perilous as dividing the last cave painting. It's a wild competition for resources that can transform friendships into a prehistoric rendition of "Survivor."

Whether it's the last piece of shell jewelry or who gets to sit closest to the fire, women have been known to battle it out. After all, economic instability and social pressures are like the original reality TV villains—they make for great drama around the communal fire pit.

But fear not! Not all cave-dwelling friendships are like a mammoth-sized soap opera. Many women prioritize solidarity and mutual respect over who has the fanciest cave decor or the shiniest rock collection. Because in the end, sharing is caring—even if it means letting someone borrow your favorite spear without asking. Whether you're forging alliances or just trying to avoid a gossip avalanche, consider solidarity and a shared mammoth feast can mend even the most torn pterodactyl hide. When betrayal does occur, it is usually related to:

Social Shenanigans: Navigating Group Chaos

Women's social circles resemble exclusive VIP clubs, where trust and intimacy are highly prized commodities. When that trust is shattered, it's akin to someone spilling the punch bowl at prom—awkward, unforgettable, and guaranteed to make waves that echo through the social jungle for eons. It's like realizing your favorite cave bear claw necklace is actually made of plastic—disappointing and a stark reminder of the fragility of social bonds in the caveman chic era.

Relationship Riddles: The People Puzzle

Ladies' connections resemble a rollercoaster of emotions—up, down, and loop-de-loop! One moment, it's a friendship feud worthy of reality TV drama, complete with dramatic confrontations and intense negotiations over who gets the last glass of virtual wine. The next, it's a heartwarming hug fest over bottomless mimosas at brunch, where grievances are forgotten faster than you can say "Extra avocado toast, please!" It's like riding through a wild theme park of social dynamics, where the rides range from thrilling to heartwarming, and sometimes a bit dizzying—but always worth the exhilarating journey.

Competing Crazies: Who's Winning Now?

In certain arenas, women can unleash their competitive spirit with more fervor than a toddler in a candy store during Halloween. Whether navigating office politics or vying for the coveted title in PTA bake-offs, it's akin to entering a high-stakes game of Monopoly—each move strategized, every decision calculated, and victory celebrated with the gusto of winning Boardwalk and Park Place. It's not just about earning a gold star; it's about proving prowess and showcasing skills honed through years of multitasking, diplomacy, and a hint of baking magic that could rival any culinary competition on television. Therefore, buckle up and roll the dice, because in this arena, the only rule is that the best woman emerges triumphant, holding the metaphorical Monopoly board high above her head, ready for the next challenge that life throws her way.

Talk Like a Pro: Communication Styles Decoded

Differences in communication styles can often lead to more misunderstandings than a mime convention on a crowded street corner. It's like attempting to send a text message to your grandma while she's still using a trusty flip phone from the early 2000s—there's a technological gap that makes conveying messages feel like decoding ancient hieroglyphs. In today's fast-paced digital world, where emojis and acronyms dominate conversations, bridging this generational divide in communication can sometimes feel as challenging as teaching a mime to speak. Each misinterpreted gesture or mistimed response can turn what was meant to be a simple chat into a comedy of errors worthy of a silent film era, where actions speak louder than words, but sometimes not in the way intended.

Culture Shock: Meeting Expectations with a Smile

Society's gossip mills and the sway of Instagram influencers can turn every girl squad outing into a red-carpet affair. Who would have thought that a casual brunch could feel as dramatic as a Hollywood premiere? With each latte sip and avocado toast bite scrutinized under the virtual spotlight, it's like navigating a paparazzi-lined sidewalk. Even choosing the right filter for a group photo becomes a strategic decision, akin to selecting the perfect gown for an awards show. The pressure to capture moments of laughter and camaraderie can sometimes overshadow the joy of simply hanging out with friends, transforming a laid-back meal into an unintentional performance art piece. Regardless of whether discussing weekend plans or debating the latest celebrity gossip, every girl squad outing can feel like stepping onto the stage of social media stardom, where even the most ordinary moments are elevated to cinematic heights.

"Navigating women's social dynamics is like riding a unicorn through a glitter storm—magical, messy, and totally worth it for the stories!"

Alright, buckle up for a journey through the social jungle gym, where trust issues and friendship dramas are as common as trying to explain TikTok to a T-Rex. Betrayal isn't a gender-exclusive sport—both men and women can trip over their cave sandals when it comes to trust. It's like trying to navigate a mammoth stampede blindfolded: messy and potentially disastrous.

Later in this chapter, we'll explore the intriguing world of the mean girl phenomenon, where Regina George from Mean Girls (2004) reigns supreme as the elegant Alpha feline. Because let's face it, high school drama can often feel like navigating a prehistoric battleground, where social status is prized more than the sharpest hunting spear. Just like early humans vying for dominance in their tribes, teenagers navigate a complex social hierarchy where popularity and influence are currency, and every interaction feels like a strategic move in the game of teenage survival.

My LGBTQ+ advocate friend and I have had some heartfelt discussions about how competition and the relentless pressure to conform can transform female friendships into a veritable Jurassic Park of emotions. It's like everyone's scrambling for the last T-Rex bone necklace in the gift shop—things can get pretty chaotic and messy. In this metaphorical dinosaur park of friendship dynamics, navigating the delicate balance between authenticity and societal expectations often feels like dodging velociraptors in tall grass, where one wrong move could lead to a full-blown T-Rex chase.

Sure, I've had my fair share of guy friendship dramas—like debating over who had the superior antler collection—but delving into female social dynamics is like attempting to wrangle a woolly mammoth on roller skates. It's a challenging endeavor, where the terrain is unpredictable, and one wrong move can send you sliding in unexpected directions. Women often face undue criticism for perceived pettiness or excessive scrutiny, yet navigating these intricate social circles is akin to mastering an ancient survival skill. It's about deciphering the unspoken rules, understanding the nuances of communication, and maintaining a delicate balance between camaraderie and competition.

But when you find your tribe amidst this wild terrain, it's like stumbling upon a life-saving invention. It's discovering fire on a cold night—it warms you from within, provides light in the darkness, and creates opportunities for sharing stories and roasting marshmallows together. Finding your tribe isn't just about fitting in; it's about forging bonds that withstand the tests of time and adversity, like a flame that continues to burn bright through the ages.

Thus, here's to navigating the treacherous waters of friendship, where whether you're a T-Rex in a tiara or a caveman with a Netflix subscription, finding solidarity and bonding over a mutual love for dinosaur memes can make all the difference.

In this jungle of social dynamics, where alliances can shift as swiftly as a saber-toothed cat stalking its prey, having friends who understand your quirks and appreciate your sense of humor is like discovering a hidden oasis. It's a refuge where you can let down your guard, share your triumphs and tribulations, and laugh over the absurdities of life—even if those absurdities sometimes feel like trying to teach a woolly mammoth ballet.

Friendship, after all, is not just about smooth sailing through calm seas; it's about weathering storms together, whether those storms involve navigating through office gossip or surviving a group chat gone rogue. It's finding someone who'll stick with you through the highs and lows, whether you're celebrating victories or commiserating over dating mishaps that feel more epic than a mammoth migration.

Here's to celebrating friendship—where whether you're bonding over brunch or supporting each other through existential crises, having a tribe that accepts you for who you are is like uncovering a treasure trove of joy in the midst of life's chaotic jungle gym. Cheers to finding your people, because with them by your side, even the murkiest waters of friendship can become a refreshing dip on a hot summer day.

"Friendships among women are like group chats: full of inside jokes, screenshots of bad Tinder dates, and debates over who gets the last piece of chocolate."

As a grown-up guy who's been fortunate to share laughs, dad jokes, and heart-to-heart moments with both my family and my lady friends, I've also had a front-row seat to witness the intricate dance of female friendship politics up close. It's akin to trying to teach calculus to a cat—utterly confusing and certainly not their strong suit!

If you've ever found yourself bewildered by the intricate ways in which women navigate the labyrinth of social dynamics—be it at home, in the neighborhood, or even in the office—allow me to shed some light on the subject. Imagine a scene where a pack of velociraptors is meticulously planning their next hunt, but instead of leaving claw marks on cave walls, emojis and group texts are flying   around faster than you can shake a tail feather!

From forming alliances based on shared interests to skillfully sidestepping the occasional stink-eye, the intricacies of cavewomen's friendships resemble navigating through a mammoth-sized jungle gym of emotions and unspoken rules. It's akin to deciphering cave drawings created with berry juice—vivid, often mysterious, and sometimes requiring a keen ear for grunts and groans to unravel the hidden meanings.

Whether you're a caveman trying to decipher the rituals of the cave squad or a cavewoman pondering why your BFF keeps rearranging the cave paintings without consulting you, here's the scoop: friendship politics have been around as long as the pursuit of a woolly mammoth. But fear not! A hearty laugh and a shared mammoth feast have always been able to smooth over any rocky social terrain, from the dawn of time to the present day.

"Women's friendships: where saying 'I hate her' can mean 'I'm insanely jealous of her outfit,' 'She forgot my birthday last year,' or 'We're basically sisters."

Ah, the delicate dance of female friendship dynamics—I've observed it from the sidelines like a caveman witnessing the invention of fire. As a guy, I've always gravitated toward the outskirts of cliques and groups. You could call it being introverted with extroverted tendencies, or simply having a knack for steering clear of drama like a T-Rex avoids meteor showers.

My circle of friends is a motley crew—childhood buddies who still share my stash of comics, neighbors who perpetually borrow my tools (and sometimes return them), and colleagues who humor me when I delve into my nerdy science jargon. It's like having a diverse buffet of friendships where everyone brings something unique to the table, even if they occasionally swipe the last piece of mammoth meat.

Now, don't get me wrong—I'm all for embracing the quirky aspects of people, even if some quirks are as persistent as a woolly mammoth during rush hour. But toxic vibes? Ain't nobody got time for that! I'd rather discuss quantum physics with a caveman than waste energy on negativity. When it's time to celebrate victories, I'm the ultimate cheerleader of friendship. Whether you're a multitasking mom conquering chaos or a scientist on the brink of curing cave bear allergies, count me in for the victory dance.

But let's delve into the intricacies of communication—because understanding each other is as vital as realizing fire doesn't taste like mammoth steak. I've learned from navigating tough conversations, like explaining to my sister that I've outgrown my childhood antics, that respect and honesty are the adhesives that keep relationships (and the occasional woolly mammoth rug) intact.

And let's not overlook the distinct challenges women navigate in the social arena. While men may boast about who unearthed the largest dinosaur bone, women have honed the art of subtle (and not-so-subtle) maneuvers. It's akin to observing a strategic battle of spear-throwing, except the weapons are words and the skirmishes include plenty of side-eye. So here's to grasping, celebrating, and sometimes sidestepping social landmines like a seasoned pro. Because in the grand saga of prehistoric friendships, every caveman and cavewoman deserves a tribe that cheers them on—even if they occasionally pilfer your prized berry stash.

"Why do Cavemen think grunting is an effective communication strategy, and why do Cavewomen have a sixth sense for finding lost socks? It's like we're living in a prehistoric sitcom!"

Ah, the intricate dance of gender dynamics—trying to herd pterodactyls during mating season would likely be less challenging! Embracing our differences is like unraveling the mystery of why dinosaurs wore feather boas—everyone brings their unique flair to the table, whether it's battling through T-Rex-sized obstacles or mastering the art of pterodactyl diplomacy.

Now, onto the fascinating realm of female friendships. It's like being in the front row at a saber-toothed soap opera, complete with twists, turns, and occasional drama over who snagged the last coconut smoothie. Women approach friendships with the strategic finesse of planning a mammoth hunt—knowing where to position oneself and whom to align with can be as crucial as navigating the tangled vines of a jungle gym.

Understanding these dynamics isn't just about decoding the intricacies of prehistoric social networks but also appreciating how these dynamics persist in modern times. From the silent signals exchanged like ancient cave paintings to the roaring discussions reminiscent of a woolly mammoth stampede, each interaction is steeped in history and evolution—both biological and social. It's about recognizing that behind every mammoth-sized challenge lies an opportunity to strengthen bonds, share laughter, and navigate the treacherous waters of social interaction with finesse and humor.

I've seen firsthand how a seemingly innocent comment can ripple through the social jungle gym faster than a T-Rex chasing its tail. In every group,   an Alpha is calling the shots, a few Betas doing damage control, and the rest just trying to avoid becoming dinosaur bait.

Hence, here's to understanding the complexities of the female hierarchy—because deciphering who's in charge is as tricky as interpreting cave paintings. Just remember, whether you're roaring like a boss T-Rex or playing it cool like a sauropod in sunglasses, embracing each other's strengths is what makes the Stone Age rock on.

Ah, the rollercoaster ride of female friendships—it's like navigating a cave maze blindfolded, hoping you don't bump into a stalactite or a drama-filled surprise. As a guy trying to decipher the mysteries of friendship dynamics, I've learned that understanding women's friendships is like trying to understand why velociraptors didn't play well with others.

Watching female friendships evolve is like watching a lava lamp— mesmerizing yet occasionally explosive. From subtle hints disguised as compliments to backhanded compliments disguised as subtle hints, it's a linguistic minefield out there.

I once had a high school friend confess; she thought gossiping made her a better friend. Thirty years later, she's still regretting it   . It's a lesson that time doesn't just fly—it swoops in like a pterodactyl, reminding us of all the social missteps we wish we could bury deeper than a woolly mammoth's footprint.

Here's to navigating the emotional T-Rex of female friendships, where forgiveness is harder to earn than a dinosaur's trust fall. Because in the end, whether you're a caveman or a cave queen, we're all just trying to avoid getting squashed by life's Jurassic-sized regrets.

When it comes to friendships, women bring the spice to life's caveman stew. I've always treasured my guy pals, but let's face it—my female friends add the extra pterodactyl wings to my social flavor.

In the prehistoric jungle of relationships, women's friendships unfold like a mesmerizing tango with a cave bear—equal parts strategic alliance and jungle warfare. It's as if each interaction is a carefully choreographed dance, where every step is planned with the precision of a cavewoman crafting the perfect spear. Meanwhile, us guys are still figuring out the basics, like how to build a decent fire without singeing our eyebrows.

Women seem to possess an innate ability to weave intricate webs of trust, support, and occasional rivalry, much like ancient hunters strategizing the best approach to take down a mammoth. They effortlessly navigate the complex social terrain, knowing when to extend an olive branch or sharpen their claws, all while maintaining the delicate balance between camaraderie and competition.

It's like observing a high-stakes game of survival where alliances shift like shifting tectonic plates, and every interaction is a potential turning point. While men may focus on straightforward tasks like honing their spear-throwing skills or scavenging for the next meal, women master the art of subtle gestures and unspoken communication, akin to deciphering the secrets hidden in cave paintings.

Understanding the intricacies of these friendships is like unraveling the mysteries of a forgotten language—each gesture, each glance, holds deeper meaning and significance. It's not just about camaraderie; it's about the evolution of social dynamics, from the ancient savannas to the bustling streets of modern cities, where the rules may have changed, but the essence of human connection remains as primal and captivating as ever.

While I'm busy trying not to step on social landmines, my female friends are mastering the art of emotional acrobatics. They want to be seen, heard, and celebrated like a T-Rex sighting in a fossil museum. Meanwhile, us guys are just happy if our grunts and nods are interpreted correctly. Here's to the women who make friendship a Jurassic adventure. Whether it's competing for the last woolly rhinoceros skin handbag or celebrating each other's successes like discovering fire, they do it all with style, grace, and the occasional cave-painting critique.

Because in the end, friendships are like mammoth hunts—better with a diverse tribe who bring their own unique skills to the hunt.

Ah, explaining the intricacies of female friendships to my son was akin to embarking on a daring quest, like teaching a T-Rex how to knit—

daunting yet filled with potential. I illustrated to him that female relationships resemble a lively prehistoric dance-off, where the art of dressing to impress isn't about mammoth-hunting prowess, but rather about asserting dominance and showcasing one's status as the top T-Rex in the cave. Understanding these dynamics, I emphasized, is crucial for navigating the social jungle with confidence and respect.

In every group of ladies, there's an Alpha female—a charismatic leader who enters with the confidence of a queen, as if draped in a majestic pterodactyl feather boa. Her presence commands respect and admiration not because of material possessions like shiny stone necklaces, but due to her innate ability to make strategic and influential moves based on her personality and charisma. She navigates the social landscape with finesse, shaping interactions and alliances with the precision of a skilled diplomat in a prehistoric court.

Men and women alike might notice your outfit, but let's be real—the real MVP is your charisma and wit, not your choice of saber-toothed tiger-print loincloth. And if everyone's dressing like they're auditioning for "Jurassic Runway," well, sometimes fitting in means biting the bullet and rocking that dino-skin chic, even if it's as comfortable as a bed of thorns.

Here's to celebrating the Alpha females of the world—leading with grace, commanding with style, and proving that leadership isn't about being the loudest dinosaur in the cave. It's about showing the herd how to stomp together towards a brighter, more fashionable Stone Age.

The legend of the Alpha female—is like finding a T-Rex wearing a tiara! These fierce leaders don't just break glass ceilings; they smash them with a mammoth-sized hammer. Imagine navigating a prehistoric jungle gym of stereotypes and outdated norms, all while rocking a saber-toothed smile. Alpha females don't just survive; they thrive in competitive environments like a raptor on roller skates—graceful, powerful, and ready to pounce on any challenge.

Their stories unfold like epic quests, brimming with moments of self-discovery, empowerment, and the delicate art of juggling personal aspirations alongside professional ambitions, akin to deftly handling flaming torches in a circus act. Balancing the responsibilities of T-Rex duties while still carving out time to master the intricate art of cave painting is indeed a formidable challenge, requiring resilience and determination that rival the bravery of early adventurers exploring uncharted territories. These narratives of perseverance and growth resonate with timeless themes of courage and ambition, showcasing the enduring spirit of individuals striving to leave their mark on the world, one brushstroke at a time.

The Alpha females of the world are rewriting history—turning "you can't" into "watch me roar!" They're not just leaders; they're trailblazers, showing the world that strength comes in many forms, including a killer stegosaurus side-eye and a strategic pterodactyl pep talk.

Ah, the Alpha females—shaking up boardrooms, parliament, and the occasional saber-toothed catwalk. These trailblazers don't just break glass ceilings; they rewrite the entire Stone Age rulebook!

You'll find them commanding armies of spreadsheets, leading debates like a T-Rex leading a dinosaur choir, and turning political arenas into literal battlegrounds. They redefine norms so boldly that even the woolly mammoths are taking notes! Sure, they might ruffle a few pterodactyl feathers along the way with their assertiveness and ambition. Critics might say they've "gone Man," "butch," or even "slept their way to the top," but let's be real—when you're rewriting history, there's bound to be some jealous dino-drama.

These Alpha females are just rocking their T-Rex power poses and showing everyone that leadership isn't about gender—it's about raw talent, determination, and the occasional Jurassic-level sass. Here's to the ladies who roar louder than a T-Rex with a megaphone—paving the way for equality and proving that leadership skills are as timeless as a stegosaurus sunset.

Ah, the ancient myth of successful women "going man," "becoming butch," or "sleeping   their way to the top"—it's akin to believing T-Rexes strutted around in high heels! These outdated stereotypes are as irrelevant as trying to hunt a woolly mammoth with a stick. Today, women are rewriting these narratives with each stride toward equality, proving that strength and success come in all forms, regardless of outdated perceptions.

Let's face it, folks. When a woman climbs the ladder of success, critics sometimes grasp for explanations that feel more prehistoric than a cave painting. It's like suggesting a pterodactyl learned to crochet—it simply doesn't add up! These outdated attempts to undermine female achievements only highlight the need for a modern perspective that celebrates diversity and recognizes the multifaceted strengths women bring to every endeavor.

These claims reflect antiquated gender biases that seem better suited to the Stone Age than to today's world of T-Rex CEOs and brontosaurus brain surgeons. Let's raise a toast to smashing stereotypes like a stegosaurus breaking rocks—because when women excel, it's not about "going man," but about forging their own path to greatness. It's about recognizing and celebrating the diverse talents and capabilities that women bring to every field and industry, breaking down barriers and reshaping perceptions along the way. Here are a few reasons why these claims persist:

Stereotyping Gender: Breaking Down the Myths

Here's the caveman perspective on all this fuss about leadership traits: it's like suggesting that only the mammoth hunters have what it takes to lead the tribe, relegating the berry pickers to mere berry picking. But what if a berry picker proves they can outsmart a cave bear with their cunning and resourcefulness? It's high time we reconsider those old cave drawings!

In the Stone Age, survival depended on diverse skills and quick thinking, not just brute strength. A leader who can strategize, innovate, and adapt—whether they're hunting mammoths or gathering berries—could be the key to the tribe's prosperity and safety. It's about recognizing that leadership isn't defined by traditional roles alone but by the ability to inspire, protect, and guide the community toward a prosperous future.

Imagine a tribe where everyone's unique talents are valued and leveraged for the greater good—where the wisdom of the berry picker is as respected as the bravery of the mammoth hunter. Embracing diversity in leadership means embracing the full spectrum of human potential, challenging outdated notions, and paving the way for a more inclusive and dynamic tribe.

Gender Double Standards: Ridiculous or Just Ridiculous?

When a cavewoman steps up as a leader, it's like igniting a volcanic eruption of scrutiny and gossip. Every decision she makes is dissected and debated: did she lead the mammoth hunt because of her charm, her spear skills, or something else entirely? Meanwhile, the caveman leader seems to swing his club with impunity, and his actions are rarely subjected to the same level of scrutiny.

The dynamics of leadership in the Stone Age are a reflection of deeper societal biases and expectations. Cavewomen who exhibited strong leadership qualities faced scrutiny and criticism that their male counterparts did not. Her assertiveness might be misinterpreted as aggression, while a caveman displaying similar traits would be lauded for his strength and decisiveness.

Yet, despite the whispers and doubts, the cavewoman's roar serves a crucial purpose. It rallies the tribe, instills courage, and guides them through challenges like a beacon in the darkness of uncertainty. Her leadership is not just about asserting dominance but about ensuring the survival and prosperity of the community in the harsh prehistoric world.

Over time, as the tribe witnesses the effectiveness of her leadership, perceptions begin to shift. The tribe comes to recognize that her strength lies not just in her physical prowess but in her ability to unite and guide them. Ultimately, her roar becomes a symbol of resilience, determination, and the evolving understanding that leadership knows no gender—just as a mammoth's worth is not solely defined by its tusks but by the strength and wisdom it brings to the tribe.

Beyond the Wheel: Rethinking Leadership in the Stone Age

You know what really grinds my stones? It's the persistent justification for inequality by claiming cavewomen aren't fit for leadership simply because they didn't invent the wheel. But let's be factual here—while the cavemen were busy obsessing over rolling stones, cavewomen were mastering the art of spear-throwing with a precision that could rival any mammoth hunt. It's like saying a saber-toothed tiger isn't a formidable predator just because it doesn't roar like a mammoth.

In the harsh and unpredictable landscape of the Stone Age, survival depended on adaptability and skill. Cavewomen honed their abilities in hunting, gathering, and defending their tribes, demonstrating resilience and strategic thinking in every aspect of their lives. Leadership wasn't about who invented what; it was about who could lead the tribe through the challenges of their environment.

When critics dismiss cavewomen's leadership potential because they didn't invent a particular tool or technology, they overlook their invaluable contributions to the tribe's survival. It's akin to judging a fish by its ability to climb a tree instead of its prowess in swimming upstream. Leadership in the ancient world was multifaceted, requiring not just innovation but also courage, resourcefulness, and the ability to inspire and unite others in times of adversity.

In today's context, it's crucial to recognize and celebrate the diverse strengths and qualities that each gender brings to leadership. Just as cavewomen's skills in spear-throwing were vital for their communities' survival, modern leadership demands a recognition of the full spectrum of talents and capabilities, irrespective of gender stereotypes or historical inventions. After all, leadership isn't about who came first—it's about who can lead best.

The stories we weave around the campfire have a profound impact on our perceptions of the world. When the cave paintings depict only successful cavewomen gossiping about berries, it perpetuates the stereotype that they aren't capable of the grand mammoth hunts or leadership roles. It's like judging a saber-toothed tiger by its purr rather than its roar—a gross oversimplification.

To challenge these stereotypical narratives, we need to update the cave walls with stories that celebrate real leadership and daring feats. Cavewomen weren't just bystanders in their communities; they were integral to survival, wielding spears with precision and guiding their tribes through challenges with resilience and strategic acumen. Their contributions deserve to be etched alongside those of cavemen, showcasing the diversity of skills and roles within early societies.

By highlighting stories of cavewomen leading hunts, making critical decisions, and fostering unity, we can inspire future generations to see leadership as a multifaceted trait that transcends gender stereotypes. It's about recognizing and celebrating the full spectrum of capabilities that each member of the tribe brought to the table, regardless of outdated narratives or simplistic depictions in ancient art.

As we update our narratives, we not only honor the legacy of cavewomen but also pave the way for a more inclusive and equitable understanding of leadership in our own times. Just as the campfire stories shaped perceptions in the past, our stories today have the power to shape a future where everyone's potential is recognized and celebrated.

It's time to shatter these antiquated stone-age stereotypes and level the playing field for every cavewoman to have a fair chance at leading the tribe. Who decided   only the cave chiefs could paint their dreams on the cave walls anyway? It's like saying only the best spear throwers can aim for the stars, while the rest are left in the shadows.

Imagine a tribe where all cavewoman's strengths and aspirations are celebrated, where leadership isn't confined to a single gender role but is recognized in all its diverse forms. From mastering the art of gathering medicinal herbs to strategizing for mammoth hunts, cavewomen have always displayed leadership qualities that are just as vital as those of the cave chiefs. It's about time we rewrite the narrative on the cave walls to reflect the true diversity of skills and contributions within our communities.

By embracing a more inclusive view of leadership, we empower cavewomen to step into roles that historically may have been reserved for their male counterparts. Whether it's guiding the tribe through times of scarcity or fostering innovation in toolmaking, every cavewoman deserves the opportunity to showcase her talents and lead with vision and strength.

Let's erase the limitations imposed by outdated stereotypes and paint a new picture of leadership—one where cave walls tell stories of courage, resilience, and determination, regardless of gender. Together, we can create a tribe where everyone's dreams and ambitions are valued, and where each cavewoman can proudly leave her mark on history, one cave painting at a time.

Ultimately, these claims about successful women "going man," "becoming butch," or "sleeping   their way to the top" are like trying to explain a T-Rex using a smartphone—it's just plain absurd! These notions reflect ancient societal attitudes towards gender roles and power dynamics, as outdated as trying to tame a velociraptor with a salad.

Sure, successful women might face these dino-sized challenges in their careers, but let's be real—gender equality isn't about who can wrestle a mammoth or who has the fanciest stone necklace. It's about recognizing and challenging these biases so that everyone—dinosaurs included—can thrive based on their skills, talents, and contributions.

Here's to smashing stereotypes like a meteor hitting the Earth—because when it comes to professional success, it's not about "going man," it's about evolving beyond outdated beliefs and unleashing the true T-Rex power of talent and determination. Successful women may experience loneliness at the top for several reasons:

Isolation in Female Leadership: Challenges and Solutions

The underrepresentation of women in leadership positions often creates a challenging environment where female leaders may find themselves lacking peers who truly understand the unique challenges and pressures they face. This sense of isolation can be profound and impactful.

Navigating the landscape of leadership can already be daunting, but when there are few women in similar roles, the opportunity for shared experiences and support networks becomes limited. Without peers who can relate to their specific struggles—whether it's dealing with gender biases, balancing work and family life, or breaking through glass ceilings—female leaders may feel isolated and unsupported.

Furthermore, this isolation can contribute to a sense of being misunderstood or undervalued in their leadership capacities. When peers and colleagues are predominantly male, it can be difficult for women to find mentors who can provide relevant guidance and advice tailored to their experiences.

To address these challenges, it's crucial to actively promote and support the advancement of women into leadership roles. Creating mentorship programs, networking opportunities, and support groups specifically for female leaders can help mitigate feelings of isolation and provide a platform for sharing experiences, strategies, and solutions.

Ultimately, by increasing the representation of women in leadership and fostering inclusive environments where their voices are heard and valued, organizations can cultivate a more supportive and empowering culture for all leaders, regardless of gender. This not only benefits individual women in leadership positions but also contributes to the overall diversity and effectiveness of leadership teams.

Work-Life Juggle: Finding Balance

Balancing demanding careers with personal life presents a formidable challenge for many successful women. The dedication required to achieve career goals often means sacrificing leisure time that could be spent socializing or nurturing personal relationships. This imbalance can lead to feelings of isolation or guilt for not being able to allocate enough time to family and friends. Despite these challenges, many women find ways to prioritize self-care and maintain meaningful connections amidst their professional pursuits, leveraging technology and strategic scheduling to stay connected with loved ones.

Perceptions and Stereotypes

Successful women often encounter stereotypes or judgments that can impact their personal relationships. Some may be seen as intimidating due to their confidence and focus on their careers, which can create barriers to   forming deeper connections with others. These perceptions may lead to misunderstandings or assumptions about their priorities, making it challenging to cultivate relationships based on mutual understanding and respect. Despite these stereotypes, many successful women actively work to break down barriers and demonstrate their ability to balance career success with meaningful personal connections.

Success, Relationships, and Societal Pressure on Women

Society frequently imposes expectations on women to fulfill caregiving roles and maintain strong social connections, alongside their professional aspirations. When women achieve success in their careers, these achievements can sometimes alter social dynamics or create new expectations that may strain existing relationships. The balance between career ambitions and societal expectations of nurturing and maintaining social connections can pose challenges for successful women, requiring them to navigate these pressures while maintaining authenticity and fulfillment in their personal lives. Despite these challenges, many women navigate these complexities with resilience and continue to redefine societal norms around success and relationships.

Navigating Leadership: Balancing Pressures and Seeking Support

The responsibilities and pressures that come with leadership roles can indeed be intense and all-consuming. Balancing the demands of decision-making, strategic planning, and overseeing teams can lead to feelings of isolation, especially when faced with difficult choices or challenges. Without a robust support network of peers who understand the complexities of leadership, it can be challenging to find the necessary guidance, empathy, and perspective to navigate these responsibilities effectively. However, many leaders actively seek out mentors, colleagues, or professional networks to lean on for support, advice, and camaraderie during times of stress or uncertainty.

Embracing Vulnerability in Competitive Environments

In competitive environments, there is often a prevailing belief that displaying vulnerability or admitting to needing support may be perceived as a weakness or a sign of inadequacy. As a result, successful women in such environments may hesitate to openly discuss their challenges or seek assistance, fearing it could undermine their perceived competence or leadership capabilities. This pressure to maintain a facade of strength and self-sufficiency can create a barrier to forming authentic connections and receiving the support needed to navigate professional and personal challenges effectively. However, cultivating a culture that values vulnerability and acknowledges the complexities of leadership can help break down these barriers and foster environments where all individuals feel empowered to seek and offer support without fear of judgment.

Balancing Success and Sacrifice: Navigating Personal Commitments

Achieving success often demands significant personal sacrifices, such as long hours at work, frequent travel, and the necessity to prioritize professional commitments over personal ones. These sacrifices can strain personal relationships, leading to feelings of loneliness and isolation, especially when friends and family members may not fully understand or empathize with the demands of the journey to success. Moreover, the pressure to maintain high standards and meet ambitious goals can consume much of one's time and energy, leaving little room for nurturing and sustaining personal connections. Despite these challenges, many successful individuals find ways to strike a balance and cultivate meaningful relationships that provide them with support and fulfillment outside of work.

It's important to recognize that success manifests differently for each woman, much like how each stegosaurus had a distinctive arrangement of plates and tail spikes. While some may prioritize their careers intensely, others might navigate a more balanced approach, integrating personal passions and relationships alongside professional achievements. Each woman's journey reflects her values, ambitions, and the resources available to her, shaping her path toward success in diverse and often unexpected ways. Ultimately, celebrating this diversity in approaches and outcomes contributes to a more inclusive and supportive environment for all women striving to achieve their goals. Each woman's journey is as unique as a stegosaurus with a personalized tail spike!

But seriously, tackling these challenges can create ecosystems where successful women aren't just surviving—they're thriving like velociraptors in a free-range buffet. Let's build workplaces where T-Rex CEOs can roar with confidence and high-five pterodactyl interns without fear of being labeled as "too ambitious" or "not dino-friendly enough." Because when it comes to supporting successful women, let's ditch the outdated notions faster than a comet zooming toward Earth. It's time to create environments where everyone can unleash their inner T-Rex of talent and rule the dino-world with flair!

Fashion Tips from Cavewomen: The Stone Age Style Guide

Ah, the eternal dance of caveman genes and modern fashion faux pas! Ladies, your choice of attire might unwittingly unleash a Jurassic Park of thoughts in the minds of men. Some dress to impress, while others are just trying to survive the fashion meteor shower. But let's be real, fellas—it's not about the dino-print leggings or the mammoth fur mini-skirt. Men, take note: we're talking about appreciating the whole package, not just the T-Rex t-shirt. Authenticity is key! Show off your beliefs, humor, and hobbies like a diplodocus showing off its neck—because that's what really gets the lava bubbling in a man's heart.

And let's not forget, ladies—kindness is the triceratops horn of attractiveness. It's like discovering a hidden cave of gold in a sea of cave bears. Plus, humor? It's like finding a pterodactyl egg in your morning omelet—unexpectedly delightful and oh-so-appealing.

Whether you're rocking a dino onesie or a pterodactyl feather boa, remember: it's your personality that leaves a Jurassic-sized footprint, not just your wardrobe choices. And that's the paleontological truth, my friends!

Ah, the mating dance of the clever man, using his wit like a caveman used his spear—except now, it's to snag a mate instead of a mammoth! And ladies, let's talk dress code: your outfit isn't just a fashion statement; it's a full-blown Jurassic Park experience for the eyes of men. Sure, showing some skin might attract attention, but beware of those T-Rexes lurking around who only see the surface! Focus on your inner diplodocus—kindness, personality, and skills that make men roar with admiration.

Because let's face it, ladies: you're not just a fashion exhibit; you're a full-fledged T-Rex of awesome qualities waiting to be discovered. Beyond appearances, your strengths, intelligence, and unique talents make you formidable and fascinating. Men, take note: compliments should be like finding a pterodactyl egg—rare, precious, and genuinely appreciated. They should uplift and acknowledge without any strings attached or expectations of reciprocation. Celebrating each other's qualities and achievements creates a supportive and empowering dynamic where everyone can thrive and shine.

Whether you're rocking a dino-print dress or a saber-toothed tiger print, remember: respect is the triceratops horn of admiration, a sturdy and essential trait. Kindness, on the other hand, acts like the stegosaurus tail of attraction, drawing people closer with its gentle but effective gestures. Let's leave behind the caveman antics of the past and embrace a future where everyone celebrates and appreciates each other for the T-Rex-sized awesomeness they bring to the table!

And scholars, they've theorized that marriage was humanity's original security system—because let's face it, in caveman times, you needed a mate who could wrestle a woolly mammoth just as much as you needed someone to share the cave with! Here's to the evolution of dating from mammoth hunting to modern-day Tinder swiping, where the struggle for love and mammoth meat continues—because hey, some things never change, even if the furs and fire have been swapped for fancy clothes and smartphones!

"No matter how hot she looks, there is a guy out there who is sick of her shit."
Opposite of that statement, "No matter how handsome he appears, there's a woman out there who's tired of his nonsense."

Cavewomen Cliques: Navigating the Prehistoric Friendships

Imagine a world where every girl's night out was secretly a scientific experiment in hormone therapy! Ladies, did you know that your bestie is your personal oxytocin dispenser? Yep, forget pharmacies—just call up your BFF for a healthy dose of the "love hormone"! These platonic bonds aren't just about giggles and gossip; they're a full-blown biochemical support system. Who needs a therapist when you've got serotonin and dopamine on speed dial? Every laugh shared and secret whispered triggers a cascade of feel-good chemicals that can brighten the darkest days.

And let's not forget the power of a good hug—better than any multivitamin! When you embrace your friends, your brain releases a flood of oxytocin, instantly lifting your spirits and strengthening your bond. It's like a warm, fuzzy force field against stress and anxiety. Next time you're feeling blue, don't reach for the chocolate; reach out to your gal pals. They're not just your friends; they're your emotional SWAT team, ready to boost your well-being and fend off loneliness with a barrage of oxytocin-fueled love bombs!

These friendships act like a built-in wellness program, delivering mood-boosting benefits without any prescription needed. Whether it's a spontaneous dance party in the living room or a heartfelt chat over coffee, your girlfriends are your personal happiness squad. They come equipped with endless supplies of laughter, empathy, and support, making them the ultimate antidote to life's challenges. Moreover, embrace the magic of these connections, and let your friends shower you with the best kind of therapy—one that's free, fun, and fabulously effective.

The Mean Cavewoman: Drama in the Stone Age!

The secret life of mean girls—like spies in a high school drama! These relational ninjas have perfected the art of social espionage from their preteen years straight through adulthood. Who knew that behind that innocent smile and attentive ear lurked a master manipulator ready to drop a gossip bomb? It's like a covert operation of emotional espionage. They'll cozy up, gather intel on your deepest secrets, and then—bam!—use it against you like a secret weapon in their quest for social dominance. Forget James Bond; these ladies are the real secret agents of the lunchroom!

And guess what? They're not just mean; they're strategic. They've honed their skills through years of practice, blending in with the crowd until they strike with all the subtlety of a glitter bomb at prom. From orchestrating elaborate exclusion tactics to spreading rumors with the precision of a viral marketer, their methods are as calculated as a chess game. Each move is carefully planned to maintain their position at the top of the social hierarchy, making sure no one dares to challenge their reign.

These mean girls are masters of psychological warfare, employing tactics that would make Machiavelli proud. They'll throw a compliment your way, just to disarm you, then unleash their true intentions when you least expect it. Their ability to manipulate social dynamics is almost an art form—turning friends into foes and allies into adversaries with just a few well-placed words.

When someone offers you a sympathetic ear, beware: it might just be a mean girl in disguise, plotting her next move in the battle for cafeteria supremacy! They're like social chameleons, adept at changing their colors to blend in seamlessly, all while scheming their next strategic attack. In this high-stakes game of popularity, it's always good to stay vigilant—because you never know when a seemingly friendly smile might hide a cunning, glitter-bomb-wielding adversary. Relational aggression is a type of behavior aimed at damaging someone's social relationships or status through covert tactics like gossip, exclusion, and manipulation; this can include:

Social Climbing: Status and Power Plays

In the ancient cavewoman's world, gossip was the ultimate power play—a way to paint the cave walls with stories that kept everyone talking, speculating on who was in and who was out. It wasn't just idle chatter; gossip shaped alliances, influenced decisions, and determined social hierarchies, making it a potent tool for navigating the complexities of tribal life. As individuals jostled for influence and recognition, gossip became a currency of social status, revealing underlying power dynamics and the intricate web of relationships that defined their community.

Game of Frenemies: Competition and Jealousy

In the fierce arena of cavewoman society, the quest for attention often sparks metaphorical battles. Whether vying for the best cave or the affections of the most handsome caveman, these contests are marked by sharp glares and whispered grunts. Each gesture and exchange carries weight, as individuals navigate a landscape where status and recognition are prized commodities. Amidst this backdrop of rivalry, jealousy simmers, fueling both ambition and conflict as cavewomen strive to secure their place in the social hierarchy and ensure their standing in the tribe.

Tear Jerkers: Mastering Emotional Expression

For cavewomen, letting out frustrations through gossip can feel like shouting into a woolly mammoth's ear instead of trying to tame it—it's loud, messy, and might just send someone running for the hills! Gossip becomes a release valve for pent-up emotions, allowing them to vent and navigate complex social dynamics without direct confrontation. In a world where survival hinges on alliances and social bonds, gossip serves as a tool for airing grievances, asserting opinions, and even forging connections through shared sentiments. It's a primal form of communication that echoes through the caves, shaping perceptions and influencing relationships amidst the challenges of daily life.

Keeping Up with the Joneses: Social Norms and Expectations

In the bustling cave where gossip reigns supreme, navigating social games can feel akin to dodging saber-toothed tigers. If whispering behind mammoth hides is the norm, honing your gossiping skills becomes essential to staying relevant in the tribe's social fabric. These norms dictate how relationships are formed and maintained, influencing everything from alliances to decision-making. Mastery of these unspoken rules isn't just about survival; it's about thriving within the intricate web of expectations and power dynamics that define cavewoman society. Adherence to these norms can secure social standing and access to resources, while deviation can lead to exclusion and isolation—a delicate balance that shapes daily interactions and communal cohesion.

Bubble Wrap for the Soul: Self-Protection and Defense

When survival i   s at stake, cavewomen aren't afraid to bare their teeth. Defending their cave, their mammoth catch   or even their favorite berry patch can turn into a battle royale. It's all about the survival of the savviest! In the rocky landscape of social dynamics, cavewomen know how to hold their ground—whether it's through whispers or war cries. After all, in the game of caves, you win or you get stuck with the last mammoth bone!

It's like Mean Girls University out there, where every woman gets a crash course in gossip and shade-throwing! Forget Hogwarts; this is where the real magic happens in learning the art of relational aggression. They're like sponges, soaking up all the drama from their older sisters, moms, and even those gossiping teachers who should know better. And let's not forget the ultimate guru of gossip—social media! It's the modern-day oracle for learning the latest in backstabbing techniques.

But hey, if you're not part of this gossip gang, watch out! You might just become the next target in their clandestine campaign of whispers and eye rolls. It's a survival tactic in the social jungle, where alliances shift faster than you can say "Did you hear?" Buckle up, ladies, and prepare for a crash course in social espionage. Whether you're ready or not, Mean Girls University is always accepting new students—and trust me, the tuition fee is paid in drama!

Female friendships are the secret sauce of life, seasoned with empathy, unwavering support, and a sprinkle of inside jokes that only we understand. Take my colleague-turned-lifelong friend for example—we've been researching and publishing papers together for so long that we practically finish each other's hypotheses! Unlike the Cavemen, cavewomen bonds go beyond work; it's a testament to the power of shared experiences and mutual understanding.

Studies suggest that strong friendships can indeed contribute to longevity, likely due to the emotional support and camaraderie they provide. As we navigate through life's ups and downs together, from deciphering texts to dissecting dilemmas, these friendships become invaluable. By the time we reach 55, the years spent nurturing these bonds often surpass those spent in some marriages, proving that having a supportive squad can be as therapeutic as any stress ball.

Let's give a shout-out to moms who are masters at juggling schedules—more adept than circus clowns! Despite their hectic routines, they somehow find time for those precious girl-time moments. Whether it's a hurried lunch date or a marathon phone catch-up session during naptime, these interactions are crucial for preserving sanity and nurturing friendships beyond the playground.

These friendships aren't just about sharing memes and splitting the bill at brunch—they're about building a community of love and laughter.

Because let's face it, life's too short to go it alone when you can navigate it with your ride-or-die squad of gal pals by your side!

Back in Cavewomen times, a strong social network wasn't just for sharing mammoth recipes—it was survival 101! Fast forward to college, where even us cavemen learned the power of female friendships. While we're busy grunting about sports or tools, women are out there actually listening and supporting each other through life's ups and downs. It's like they've got a PhD in empathy!

But let's face it, we cavemen aren't always the best listeners. We're more into grunts and nods than heartfelt conversations. That's where having friends with solid principles and unwavering support comes in handy— whether you're a caveman or cavewoman, these friendships are like having a rock-solid cave to retreat to when life gets rocky.

And those female friendships? They're like the mammoth-sized glue that holds everything together. From celebrating victories to commiserating over saber-tooth tiger scares, these bonds are the secret ingredient to a satisfying and balanced prehistoric existence.

The Origins of Cavewoman Marriage: Rock Rings and Mammoth Drama!

Marriage for women is like a prehistoric Rubik's Cube—it's been twisted and turned throughout history for all sorts of reasons. Back in the day, it wasn't just about romance and candlelit dinners. Nope, it was about securing the mammoth meat, I mean, ensuring social and economic stability through strategic alliances between families. It was like playing Civilization with real lives!

Women were the CEOs of the household, managing everything from cave decor to child-rearing, all while making sure the family lineage stayed as strong as a mastodon. Marriage wasn't just a union; it was a legal and social status upgrade, like getting the ancient equivalent of a verified checkmark. Let's not forget about arranged marriages—talk about having your Tinder profile curated by your parents! Elders played matchmakers to safeguard economic, social, and cultural interests, kind of like the original LinkedIn connections. But hey, times have changed.

Nowadays, marriage is more about finding a partner who's into binge-watching saber-tooth tiger documentaries and sharing a cave with equal passion. It's all about love, companionship, and maybe a joint mammoth meat savings account. In all seriousness, in many ancient societies, marriage served several purposes:

Money Talks: Economic and Social Stability

In ancient times, marriage wasn't merely a romantic endeavor; it was a strategic alliance aimed at bolstering economic and social stability. Each union represented a merging of tribes, pooling resources and expertise to enhance survival prospects. Women played a pivotal role in these alliances, often serving as the linchpin that solidified relationships and secured additional resources, akin to a secret weapon in the survival game. These unions weren't just about hearts and flowers; they were pragmatic decisions aimed at strengthening community resilience and ensuring collective prosperity amidst the challenges of the prehistoric landscape. Through these partnerships, families and tribes forged bonds that transcended individual interests, fostering economic security and social cohesion essential for thriving in a harsh and unpredictable environment.

Baby Boom: Reproductive and Family Fun

Marriage in ancient times was akin to signing up for the ultimate team sport: Baby Rearing 101! Women weren't merely players; they were the coaches, referees, and MVPs in ensuring the tribe's future. Beyond the emotional bonds and companionship, marriage carried significant responsibilities tied to reproduction and family dynamics. Women bore the crucial role of nurturing and raising children, ensuring the continuation and prosperity of the tribe. This role involved multifaceted tasks—from caregiving and education to imparting cultural values and survival skills. Each child was not just a member of the family but a future contributor to the tribe's strength and resilience. Thus, marriage in prehistoric societies was a cornerstone of community survival, with women at the forefront, orchestrating the intricate dance of family and societal continuity amidst the challenges of their environment.

Cultural Quirks: Social Norms and Oddities

In the ancient world, marriage was governed by the rules depicted i n cave paintings. It meant adhering strictly to norms of fidelity, shared responsibilities, and maintaining a tidy cave. Life mirrored a sitcom where the laugh track was replaced by grunts of approval, emphasizing communal values and expectations. Marriage was not just a personal commitment but a social contract that reinforced community bonds and ensured stability. By upholding these norms, couples contributed to the cohesion and well-being of their tribe, embodying roles that were both functional and symbolic in shaping cultural identity and continuity through generations.

Legal Eagles: Property Rights for Dummies

In some ancient societies, when marriages crumbled, it was mammoth fur and cave painting custody battles! Women weren't just brides—they were the CEOs of the Stone Age, navigating legal mazes to divvy up resources, protect family treasures, and keep the cave tidy. Their prowess in property and inheritance was key to keeping the tribe's bank mammoth strong and their social status saber-tooth sharp, proving they were the ultimate cave executives in a prehistoric boardroom brawl.

Holy Moly: Religious and Spiritual Significance

Marriage ceremonies in ancient times were grand tribal gatherings, drawing everyone to witness the union of souls and participate in a mammoth-sized commitment. It was akin to signing a sacred pact with the cave spirits, binding families and tribes together under the watchful gaze of ancestral wisdom. These rituals were not just about legal unions; they held profound religious and spiritual significance, invoking blessings for fertility, prosperity, and protection. The fire lit during these ceremonies symbolized not only warmth and sustenance but also the enduring flame of community and tradition. Through marriage, individuals affirmed their place within the cosmic order, honoring ancestral spirits and ensuring continuity of cultural values and beliefs amidst the challenges of their ancient world.

In the epic saga of human history, marriage was more than just a vow—it was the blueprint for survival, sanity, and sometimes a good cave painting. Throughout history, marriage has been like that ancient artifact you find in a cave—mysterious, occasionally confusing, but always evolving. From mammoth meat alliances to LinkedIn-style arranged unions, it is clear marriage has seen it all. But hey, today, we've traded mammoth meat for mutual respect, personal choice, and equality. Marriage now is like a modern-day adventure game where you choose your own quest and hopefully find the perfect co-op partner for this crazy journey called life. Here's to evolving with the times—and hopefully leaving mammoth meat negotiations in the past!

Ultimately, these bonds are about building a community of love and laughter, because life's too short to go it alone when you can navigate it with your ride-or-die squad of gal pals by your side! Back in Cavewomen times, a strong social network wasn't just for sharing mammoth recipes—it was survival 101! Fast forward to college, where even us cavemen learned the power of female friendships. While we're busy grunting about sports or tools, women are out there actually listening and supporting each other through life's ups and downs. It's like they've got a PhD in empathy! But let's face it, we cavemen aren't always the best listeners. We're more into grunts and nods than heartfelt conversations.

That's where having friends with solid principles and unwavering support comes in handy—whether you're a caveman or cavewoman, these friendships are like having a rock-solid cave to retreat to when life gets rocky. And those female friendships? They're like the mammoth-sized glue that holds everything together. From celebrating victories to commiserating over saber-tooth tiger scares, these bonds are the secret ingredient to a satisfying and balanced prehistoric existence.

For ladies, navigating the social dynamics of female friendships is a complex and nuanced journey, filled with layers of emotional, social, and cultural intricacies. As a husband, father, and friend, I've come to appreciate these relationships' depth, recognizing that they are shaped by unique experiences and perspectives. Just as cavemen navigated the challenges of survival, modern women navigate a social landscape that can

56

often feel like a labyrinth of alliances, rivalries, and deeply rooted connections. Through observing my wife and daughter, I've witnessed the profound impact of female friendships, from the supportive bonds formed in adolescence to the enduring connections maintained throughout adulthood.

In summary, as an outsider looking in, female friendships are not just about socializing; they are vital support systems that provide emotional sustenance and resilience. They are built on trust, empathy, and mutual understanding, acting as a refuge from life's challenges. These relationships can be as fierce and loyal as they are complex, embodying a strength that rivals the most formidable prehistoric alliances. In the ever-evolving jungle of social interactions, understanding and respecting these dynamics is crucial. Female friendships, with their unique blend of camaraderie, competition, and compassion, offer invaluable insights into the human experience. So, whether it's navigating the intricacies of schoolyard politics or the complexities of adult relationships, recognizing the power and significance of these bonds is essential. After all, in the end, these friendships are the mammoth-sized glue that holds everything together, providing a sense of belonging and support that is truly irreplaceable.

Chapter 4

Bro Bonds: From Grunts to Genuine Bromance

Men's friendships can resemble a covert ops mission: a lot of grunting, strategic high-fives, and an unspoken pact to avoid discussing feelings. This book covers relationships for everyone, including those guys who feel a bit awkward around the stereotypical "Caveman" types—the ones who could probably intimidate a saber-toothed tiger with their grunts alone. These guys might have trouble fitting in socially, maybe because their idea of small talk is debating the best way to cook a mammoth. But hey, deep down, they're just ordinary dudes trying to navigate the complexities of modern social circles without accidentally clubbing someone over the head with their opinions.

"Men's friendships: where 'I got your back' means 'I'll pick you up after your third failed attempt at parallel parking."

Ever seen a guy at a party standing alone, looking like he'd rather wrestle a woolly mammoth than strike up a conversation? That's the "Caveman" type—the dude who's as comfortable with emotional expression as a T-Rex in tap shoes. He's more likely to grunt than chat about feelings, preferring to navigate social gatherings with the finesse of a boulder rolling downhill.

For guys who don't quite vibe with these rugged types, it can feel like trying to fit a square wheel on a Stone Age cart. They might feel left out, wondering if they missed the memo on grunting and chest-thumping as the preferred forms of communication. Let's face it, society's expectations for men to be all stoic and saber-toothed tiger-esque don't help. Rejection? Oh, yeah, it's real. If you're not into comparing bicep sizes or discussing the optimal beard length, you might as well be invisible.

But don't fear, this book attempts to decode the mysteries of the "Caveman," sheds light on why some guys struggle to bond with them (spoiler: it's not just because they smell like smoked mammoth) and offers tips on bridging the gap. Because who knows, maybe underneath that rugged exterior, there's a dude who just needs a friendly chat about something other than hunting tactics or club craftsmanship.

"Male friendships: where insults are a form of endearment, and bonding happens over who can chug the fastest."

Ever noticed how in every group of guys, there's always that one "guy's guy" who seems to have mastered the art of manliness like it's a competitive sport? You know, the dude who can talk football stats like he's reciting ancient poetry, or who knows every brewery within a 50-mile radius? It's like he's got a PhD in bro-logy and a minor in sports trivia.

Then there are the other guys who dip their toes into "guy's guy" territory but aren't quite Olympic-level. They might know a decent amount about cars or can grill a mean burger, but their sports knowledge fizzles out after the basic rules of baseball. They're more like the JV team in the manly Olympics, doing their best but not quite ready for prime time.

And let's not forget the rare breed of guys who seem allergic to anything traditionally "guy's guy." They'd rather discuss the latest in astrophysics or debate the merits of veganism than argue over who has the best golf swing. They're the unicorns in a herd of stallions, marching to the beat of their own, non-sports-related drum.

Whether you're the MVP of manliness or the guy who's still trying to figure out what "offside" means in soccer, there's a place for every type of guy in the wonderfully diverse ecosystem of masculinity. Generally, guy's guys share standard features like:

Bros and Mammoths: The Caveman Olympics of Bonding

When cavemen aren't out hunting mammoths or honing their spear-throwing skills, they're bonding over their favorite pastimes—whether it's chasing wild animals, debating who grilled the juiciest mammoth steak, or arguing over who threw the most mammoth-shaped rock with the perfect arc. It's like a perpetual cave Olympics, where every achievement is celebrated with hearty grunts and the occasional victory dance around the fire pit. These moments of camaraderie are more than just leisure activities; they're essential for fostering unity and prowess in the tribe, ensuring that every caveman feels like a true champion in the game of prehistoric life.

Grunt, Nod, Cheer: The Caveman Guide to Conversations

When it comes to chatting, cavemen keep it simple and to the point: they grunt about mammoth sightings, nod approvingly at the latest spear upgrades, and cheer enthusiastically whenever someone lands a big cavefish. It's a conversation style as straightforward and primal as drawing stick figures on cave walls—no frills, just essential information shared in the most caveman way possible.

Men's communication often revolves around straightforward topics that require minimal elaboration. Conversations are typically practical and goal-oriented, focusing on immediate needs and shared interests. Discussing the day's hunt, planning the next expedition, or sharing tips on tool-making are common themes. The language is direct and unadorned, with gestures and grunts often serving as effective communication tools. There's a certain efficiency in this approach, ensuring that important information is conveyed quickly and clearly.

This communication style also fosters a sense of camaraderie and mutual respect. When a caveman grunts in approval of another's spear upgrade, it's not just a casual remark; it's an acknowledgment of skill and effort. Cheering for a successful cavefish catch is a communal celebration of success, reinforcing bonds within the group. These interactions build trust and solidarity, essential for survival in the harsh, prehistoric world.

Men's communication tends to avoid emotional depth, focusing instead on tangible achievements and practical solutions. It's not about expressing feelings or delving into personal matters; it's about sharing experiences and knowledge that benefit the group. This approach creates a sense of unity and purpose, where each member's contribution is valued and recognized.

In modern times, this communication style persists in many forms. Whether it's discussing sports, gadgets, or work projects, men often prefer to keep conversations straightforward and action-oriented. The essence remains the same: sharing useful information, offering support, and celebrating each other's achievements in a way that strengthens bonds and fosters mutual respect.

While the context may have changed from hunting mammoths to navigating modern challenges, the core principles of men's communication remain rooted in simplicity and practicality. It's a timeless approach that continues to serve as the foundation for strong, effective interactions among men, ensuring that essential information is conveyed, and relationships are reinforced through shared experiences and common goals.

Roar and Rib: Caveman Comedy Central for Teasing

Sure, cavemen love to poke fun at each other—whether it's boasting about who's the top mammoth wrangler or who can start the biggest cave fire. But beyond all the chest-thumping and primal bravado, there's a sharp wit that could rival the claws of a saber-toothed tiger! Their banter is as fierce as a hunting expedition and as quick-witted as catching a fish with bare hands. In the cave, laughter echoes off the walls as they exchange jabs and jests, showcasing a comedic prowess that transcends the ages—and proving that humor was as essential to survival then as it is now.

Bros and Banter: Caveman Social Skills

When cavemen gather in their cave crew, it's a never-ending prehistoric party. They swap stories of epic hunts, share tips on mammoth-slaying techniques, and debate which cave painting deserves the most grunts of approval. It's socializing on a scale that would make even the biggest cave bear jealous, with laughter echoing off the walls and camaraderie as solid as a mammoth tusk.

Bros and Roles: How Cavemen Rock the Cave!

In caveman society, there's a code carved in stone: stick to your caveman duties or risk getting mocked like a dodo bird. Whether you're the master mammoth hunter or the firekeeper extraordinaire, straying from these roles might earn you a nickname as strange as a cave painting of a dancing mammoth.

In the world of cavemen, bonding is as primal as the urge to paint the caves with tales of triumph and laughter. Gentlemen, grab your club, sharpen your spear, and join the caveman brotherhood—it's a wild ride through history's manliest moments! It's crucial to clarify that not all Caveman types are walking around with clubs, grunting aggressively, and starting fires with their eyebrows. Sure, they might exude a bit of primal energy, but deep down, many of them are teddy bears in woolly mammoth skins—friendly, approachable, and surprisingly adept at ordering a Frappuccino.

Think of them as the lovable Neanderthals of our modern age—sometimes a bit rough around the edges, but always ready to offer a helping hand or share a laugh over a primitive meme. They may roar a little too loudly during football games or flex unnecessarily when opening pickle jars, but hey, it's all part of their charm.

Let's not judge the Caveman types too harshly. After all, they're just trying to navigate a world that sometimes feels as confusing as a cave without a GPS. And who knows? Maybe their rugged charm will come in handy when we least expect it—like when we need someone to open that stubborn jar of olives or scare away a saber-toothed squirrel.

When a Man Feels "Out of Place" Around the Stereotypical Masculine Men

Back in caveman times, this guy might've been the one always left out of the mammoth hunting party, watching from the sidelines as others strategized and celebrated their victories. When it came to spear-throwing practice, he was often picked last, his efforts met with sympathetic grunts or amused chuckles from the more skilled hunters. Despite his best efforts to fit in, he often found himself on the fringes of caveman society, navigating the challenges of being the underdog in a world where strength and prowess were prized above all else. Modern man isn't so different— social dynamics and feelings of exclusion still echo these ancient struggles today.

Pebbles and Shell Games: The Caveman with Uncommon Interests

While everyone else was grunting about mammoths and sharpening their spears, this guy was probably more interested in collecting cave shells or perfecting his rock-skipping technique. Who needs sports when you've got a knack for finding the shiniest pebbles? His unique interests set him apart in a world dominated by hunting and survival skills, often leading to puzzled looks from his fellow cavemen and the occasional teasing about his preference for beachcombing over mammoth wrestling. Despite the jests, he found joy in the simple pleasures of cave life, proving that sometimes, it's the pebble collectors who end up making waves.

Brush Strokes and Spears: The Artistic Caveman

While other cavemen were flexing their muscles and showing off their spear-throwing skills, this guy was busy perfecting his cave painting of a dancing saber-tooth tiger. Who needs to be macho when you've got an artistic flair? His cave paintings captured the imagination of the tribe, depicting scenes that brought a touch of creativity and storytelling to their rugged existence. While some raised their brows at his unconventional pursuits, others admired his ability to add color and life to the walls of their cave, showing that in a world dominated by strength and survival, artistic expression could carve out its own unique niche.

Jokester Extraordinaire: Mastering the Art of Class Clownery

While other cavemen were flexing their muscles and showing off their spear-throwing skills, this guy was busy perfecting his cave painting of a dancing saber-tooth tiger. Who needs to be macho when you've got an artistic flair? His cave paintings captured the imagination of the tribe, depicting scenes that brought a touch of creativity and storytelling to their rugged existence. While some raised their brows at his unconventional pursuits, others admired his ability to add color and life to the walls of their cave. This timeless tale reminds us that even today, amidst the fast-paced demands of modern life, artistic expression continues to carve out its unique and valued niche, enriching society with beauty, imagination, and cultural depth.

Charm Over Looks: Surviving with Style

Maybe he had a few too many close encounters with saber-toothed tigers or just wasn't blessed with the biggest club. Who needs good looks when you've got charm that can disarm even the fiercest cave bear? This unconventional caveman had a knack for winning hearts with his wit and charisma, turning awkward mammoth-hunting mishaps into hilarious campfire stories that had the whole tribe roaring with laughter. His ability to lighten the mood and diffuse tense situations made him a valued member of the community, proving that in a world where brute strength often ruled, quick wit and a warm smile could be just as effective for survival and social success.

Quiet Strength: The Shy Guy's Role in the Tribe

"The Shy Guy" refers to that caveman who preferred observing over participating in the rough-and-tumble activities of the tribe. While others honed their spear-throwing skills or competed in mammoth-hunting contests, he found solace in quieter pursuits, perhaps studying the patterns of the stars or experimenting with different types of berries. His reserved nature often meant he was overlooked during the boisterous gatherings around the fire, where stories of hunting triumphs and close encounters with wild beasts took center stage. Yet, his thoughtful observations and keen eye for detail often revealed insights that others had missed, whether it was predicting changes in weather patterns or identifying edible plants that could sustain the tribe during lean times. Despite his introverted tendencies, his contributions to the tribe were invaluable, reminding everyone that strength and survival weren't just about physical prowess, but also about wisdom, patience, and a deep connection to the natural world.

Not a Masculine Male: Rethinking Strength and Identity

Maybe he never quite mastered the art of mammoth wrestling or didn't see eye-to-eye with the tribe's warrior chief. Who needs to be traditionally masculine when you've got a heart as big as a woolly mammoth? This unconventional caveman showed his strength through kindness and empathy, forging bonds with the tribe through acts of generosity and compassion. While others boasted about their hunting trophies and prowess in battle, he quietly supported the tribe's elders and cared for the younglings, earning respect not for his brawn but for his gentle spirit and unwavering loyalty. His example challenged stereotypes, proving that true strength lies not just in physical might, but in the courage to be true to oneself and to embrace qualities that benefit the entire tribe.

Unconventional Masculinity: Celebrating Non-Traditional Role Models

While other cavemen were learning to wield clubs and hunt mammoths, this guy was raised by a clan of wise cavewomen who taught him the art of weaving and the secrets of herbal medicine. Who needs male role models when you've got a tribe of strong, savvy cavewomen?

In a world of cavemen, being different might just be the best way to shake up the cave routine and paint your own path on the walls of history. Here's to the social outcasts—may your caves be cozy, your pebbles shiny, and your jokes legendary! It's perfectly fine if someone prefers not to chill with the "guy's guys." After all, not everyone dreams of bonding over beer pong and debating the best ways to grill a steak. But let's not get too high and mighty about it—just because you're more into artisanal cheese tasting than arm-wrestling contests doesn't mean you're any less flawed.

In fact, some of us non-guy's guys might secretly envy their ability to effortlessly talk about sports stats or summon a burp that shakes the foundations of a man cave. Maybe deep down, we all want to belong to that bro-tastic world but without sacrificing our collection of vintage teacups, finding a balance between different aspects of masculinity.

Instead of feeling superior, let's recognize that we're all on a journey of bromantic discovery. And who knows? Maybe one day we'll find ourselves enjoying a deep conversation about the merits of a well-cooked steak while sipping a fine Merlot. Until then, let's just appreciate each other's quirks and toast to the diversity of masculinity—whether it's clad in flannel or a silk smoking jacket. Cheers to that!

"Friendships among cavemen are like a mammoth-sized BBQ cook-off: fierce competition over who grills the best mammoth steaks, all while sharing laughs and tales of epic hunts. But let's be real—the true victory is snagging the last cold coconut brew before the saber-toothed tigers swoop in!"

Improving Bromances: A Guide to Male Bonding

A compelling reason for a man to level up his bro-bonding skills is to create a squad that's tighter than skinny jeans after Thanksgiving dinner! Because let's face it, fellas: having a crew that's got your back is as crucial as knowing where your favorite pizza joint hides its stash of extra cheese.

Think about it—when the chips are down and you need someone to help move a couch or decode cryptic text messages from your significant other, who are you gonna call? Not Ghostbusters, my friend (although that would be epic), but your trusty gang of dudes who understand your quirks and can navigate your weird sense of humor.

Whether it's organizing a beer pong tournament or just offering a shoulder to cry on when "Avengers: Endgame" hits you in the feels for the tenth time, building those bro-mantic bridges pays off big time. In the end, a true bromance isn't just about sharing a cold one—it's about sharing life's highs, lows, and the occasional embarrassing karaoke performance of "Livin' on a Prayer." By building stronger connections with other men, individuals can:

Bromances: Bonds Stronger Than Mammoth Hide

Building bromances stronger than a mammoth's hide creates a robust support network where men forge bonds over shared experiences, from savoring the last mammoth steak to navigating the challenges of saber-toothed tiger encounters. These friendships offer camaraderie and mutual understanding, providing emotional support and a sense of belonging in the wild and unpredictable world of the cave.

The Power of Camaraderie in the Stone Age

In a world where every caveman is expected to be a lone wolf, forging strong relationships helps dismantle the cave walls of isolation. Even the toughest caveman needs a tribe to help him find his cave keys and navigate the treacherous terrain of mammoth hunts and saber-toothed tiger encounters. These bonds of camaraderie provide not just companionship, but also emotional support and shared wisdom that make surviving the challenges of prehistoric life a bit more bearable—and a lot more fun!

Fireside Bonds: The Power of Caveman Camaraderie

Turns out, exchanging grunts and groans with your cave buddies can work wonders for mammoth-sized worries. Beyond just hunting together, strong friendships among cavemen ensure the cave fires stay ablaze, fostering trust and camaraderie that withstands the harshest mammoth hunts and darkest cave nights.

Cave Networking: From Mammoth Hunts to Career Tips

Whether sharing mammoth hunting strategies or offering cave painting tips, strong friendships among cavemen open doors to the best job recommendations on this side of the lava pit. It's like attending a networking event where the only entry fee is a slab of mammoth jerky, forging connections that prove invaluable in the rugged landscape of prehistoric life.

Words Over Weapons: Building Relationships in the Stone Age

Who needs a spear when the power of words can build bridges among cavemen? Strengthening relationships leads to fewer club-swinging disagreements and more collaborative brainstorming sessions on how to outsmart the cave bear. It's about creating a supportive community where innovative ideas flourish and conflicts are resolved with wit rather than brute force.

Thriving Together: Building Supportive Bonds

By building bonfires of friendship, cavemen can show the younglings how to be the tribe's MVP. Because in caveman culture, real strength comes from sharing, not just spear-throwing. Overall, a mammoth-sized heart and a tribe of friends mean more laughs, fewer mammoth-sized problems, and a cave life filled with more high-fives than grunts of frustration. Ultimately, nurturing positive relationships among men creates a supportive environment where everyone can thrive—whether it's at home, work, or just figuring out which sports team to cheer for!

From Mammoth Hunts to Matrimony: The Origins of Marriage for Men

Sociologists, anthropologists, and scholars love to theorize about marriage's origins. One popular idea is that it all started with Cavemen flexing their muscles to protect their families and bring home mammoth meat! Yep, before roses and candle lit dinners, marriage was basically about the survival of the beefiest. Next time you're at a wedding, just picture a caveman in a tuxedo, handing out mammoth steaks instead of wedding favors!

Evidence suggests that marriage is as ancient as those stubborn socks you always lose in the dryer. Back then, families were like roaming bands of 30 people, with multiple alpha males, shared women, and all the kids— they were like the original reality TV show! When they settled down, they decided, "Hey, let's get hitched!" The first recorded wedding bells chimed around 2350 B.C. in Mesopotamia, and marriage soon spread faster than gossip at a toga party. But love and religion? Nah, back then it was all about safety, security, and making sure mammoth meat dinners weren't interrupted by saber-toothed tigers! Here are some critical aspects of the origins of marriage for men:

The Hilarious History of Social, Economic, and Marriage Alliances

Once upon a time, in a world not so far away, marriage wasn't just about love and companionship—it was the ultimate power move! Let's dive into the hilarious reasons why tying the knot was serious business.

Stone Age Strategy: Marriage as the Ultimate Power-Up

Back in the day, marriage wasn't just about finding your soulmate; it was about leveling up in society like you were in some medieval RPG. Men would strut their stuff, trying to prove they were the Elon Musk of their time, ready to provide and play politics like pros. Picture a never-ending game of Monopoly where saying "I do" was like landing on a Boardwalk with a hotel. Marriage was the ultimate power-up, giving you the keys to wealth, resources, and alliances, all while making you look like the boss of a real-life Game of Thrones. Even today, marriage often carries echoes of these ancient social and economic strategies, as people still seek partnerships that can enhance their social status, financial stability, and overall life opportunities.

Reproductive Roulette: Marriage as the Ultimate High-Stakes Poker Game

Imagine marriage as a high-stakes poker game for men's reproductive roles. It wasn't just about ensuring your genes lived on; it was about passing down the family name and that sweet inheritance. Talk about pressure! Men had to up the ante and prove they could handle the demands of being a protector and provider. It wasn't just a role; it was a full-time job with no vacation days or sick leave. Picture a medieval dad trying to teach his son how to swing a sword while also managing the family farm and fending off invaders. The stakes were high, and the expectations even higher. Failure wasn't an option because the family's future and fortune were on the line. This is as true today as it was 12,000 years ago: societal expectations often pressure men to be the primary providers and protectors, balancing career demands with family responsibilities to ensure financial security and continuity.

Legal Limbo: The Rollercoaster Ride of Ancient Marriage

In some cultures, marriage wasn't just about saying "I do." It was a legal rollercoaster that gave men rights to property, inheritance, and the keys to the kingdom (or at least the house). Marriage contracts were less about love and more about land, livestock, and lineage. Think of it as a medieval version of Shark Tank, where potential grooms pitched their worthiness to win the ultimate investment: a bride.

Being the head of the household meant making all the big decisions, like whether to upgrade to a moat or invest in a new catapult, not to mention choosing between planting wheat or barley, and figuring out how to fend off those pesky rival clans. It was like being the CEO of a medieval startup, where every choice could make or break the family fortune.

And let's not forget the labyrinth of laws and customs that had to be navigated—one wrong move and you could lose your castle faster than you can say "pre-nup." Marriage was less of a romantic union and more of a strategic partnership, complete with a hefty dose of legalese thrown in for good measure. If you thought modern marriage was complicated, just imagine trying to balance love, livestock, and land while dodging arrows and legal loopholes. Modern marriage often involves navigating complex legalities and shared responsibilities as our Stone Age relatives. Both men and women balance careers, ambitions, and household management to build a stable and prosperous family life.

Cultural Curtain Calls: Navigating Marriage in the Spotlight

Cultural norms were the ultimate puppet masters, pulling the strings on everything from fidelity expectations to who got to be the chief chef at the annual village barbecue. Marriage wasn't just about two people; it was about fitting into the mold society carved out for you. Imagine living in a world where stepping out of line could land you on the village gossip circuit faster than you can say "scandal."

Forget about personal preferences—if your culture said you had to wear matching goat-skin outfits every Tuesday, you better believe you'd be rocking that look. Want to be a stay-at-home dad? Good luck with that, unless you enjoy being the subject of endless jokes at the tavern. And don't even think about suggesting a potluck for the village barbecue; everyone knows that the role of the chief chef was passed down from generation to generation, like an heirloom ladle.

Marriage meant playing your part to perfection in the grand performance of societal expectations. Deviate from the script, and you'd get more than just side-eye—you'd get the full village theater experience, complete with dramatic sighs, disapproving whispers, and possibly public shaming. You learned your lines, hit your marks, and hoped that someday the curtain would fall on the rigid rules, giving way to a more improvisational approach to love and life. Modern men and women often face societal pressures to conform to cultural norms and expectations in their relationships, balancing personal desires with the roles and behaviors deemed acceptable by their communities.

Divine Drama: The Celestial Spectacle of Ancient Marriage

Last but not least, marriage had a divine flair—it was like getting hitched and blessed by the entire celestial team. Imagine your wedding as the ultimate crossover episode where the gods themselves made a guest appearance. Religious ceremonies weren't just for show; they added a sprinkle of spiritual significance, making sure everyone knew this wasn't just a union of two hearts but a pact approved by the big guy upstairs.

Picture this: you're standing at the altar, and instead of just your Aunt Mildred watching, you've got Zeus, Odin, and a whole host of deities giving their celestial nod of approval. The officiant wasn't just any old priest; he was the divine hype man, making sure the universe knew this marriage was legit. Forget about simply exchanging rings—you might have had to perform a sacred dance, sacrifice a goat, or endure an epic blessing that could rival a Shakespearean monologue.

The pressure was real. You weren't just trying to impress your in-laws; you were trying to get a thumbs up from the gods themselves. Step out of line, and you might find yourself dealing with divine disapproval—think thunderbolts, plagues, or an unfortunate transformation into a pillar of salt. You put on your best tunic, smiled through the ritual chants, and hoped that the divine audience appreciated your performance.

Marriage wasn't just a social contract; it was a celestial endorsement with divine VIPs watching your every move. Sure, today's weddings might feature bridezillas and overbearing mothers-in-law, but at least you don't have to worry about offending Zeus or having Thor crash your reception with a thunderbolt. Imagine the stress of making sure your union met divine standards, lest you end up cursed with bad luck or turned into a goat. Thankfully, modern weddings are more about dodging crazy relatives than dodging divine retribution, making the journey to the altar a bit less fraught with supernatural peril.

Overall, the origins of marriage for men are like a recipe passed down through generations: a complex blend of social spices, economic seasoning, cultural flavors, and just a pinch of religious herbs. Over the centuries, these ingredients have simmered together, creating a stew that shapes personal identity, family dynamics, and society's taste buds. Whether you're into traditional dishes or modern fusion cuisine, marriage continues to be a dish served with a side of deep-rooted expectations and a dash of "happily ever after."

Next time you hear someone say marriage is a walk in the park, remind them it used to be more like navigating a medieval maze full of traps, treasures, and the occasional dragon. Cheers to love, laughter, and the quest for that perfect alliance!

The Male Dress Code: Fashion Faux Pas Through the Ages

The "Male Dress Code" is like a confusing recipe with too many ingredients—societal norms, cultural expectations, and fashion rules all mixed into one potluck of attire advice for men. It's like trying to follow a recipe with instructions that keep changing depending on whether you're at work, at a wedding, or just grabbing groceries. One minute, you're told to dress business casual, and the next, you're deciphering the difference between cocktail attire and semi-formal.

Navigating through this maze of sartorial guidelines can feel like you're solving a puzzle where the pieces keep shifting. One wrong move, and you're either overdressed or underdressed, looking like you took a wrong turn in the wardrobe department. If you've ever wondered why dressing up sometimes feels like navigating through a labyrinth, blame it on the ever-evolving "Male Dress Code" that has more twists and turns than a mystery novel. Each social scenario comes with its own set of unwritten rules, turning what should be a simple task into a complex challenge.

Fashion Police Alert: The Male Dress Code Debacle

In the grand scheme of societal norms, men are expected to dress like they're ready to seal a business deal or rescue a kitten from a tree—functionality first, fashion second. Provocative attire? That's like wearing a "kick me" sign to a board meeting. Who needs distractions when you're trying to impress with your PowerPoint skills? Okay, gents, keep those flashy outfits in the closet and stick to the script: business casual or heroic rescuer, no exceptions!

Dress for Success, Not for Laughs

Picture this: you're at a networking event, trying to pitch your brilliant startup idea, and someone walks in wearing a neon pink crop top and denim cutoffs. Professionalism just took a nosedive faster than a bad stock market day. Men know better than to gamble their reputation on a wardrobe malfunction. It's all about looking sharp and staying classy because no one wants to be remembered as the guy who dressed like a fashion disaster at the most important meeting of his life.

Comfort is King, Fashion is Queen

Let's be real—most guys aren't dreaming of strutting around in feather boas or skintight spandex. They prefer clothing that's as reliable as their Netflix queue—practical, predictable, and doesn't require a degree in contortionism to put on. Comfort over couture, any day of the week, because who needs a fashion statement when you can have sweatpants that feel like a hug from a cloud?

Culture Clash Couture: When Traditions Go Trendy

When tradition and religion chime in, men heed the call to keep things modest. There's no need to upset Aunt Mildred at the family reunion with an outfit that could rival a Vegas showgirl. Respect the culture, avoid the side-eye, and keep it classy.

Macho Machinations

For some fellas, provocative clothes might as well be labeled "Exit Only." They'd rather flex their biceps or rock a beard that screams "I chop wood for breakfast" than risk looking like they accidentally raided their sister's closet. Confidence and competence—now that's the real macho manifesto.

Safety First, Style Second: Fashionably Secure

Let's not forget the ultimate buzzkill—safety concerns. Wearing provocative gear could turn heads for all the wrong reasons. Who needs unwanted attention or a catcall when all you wanted was a latte in peace? Men stick to attire that keeps the focus on their charm, not their calves—because the only thing worse than spilling hot coffee is dodging unwanted advances in tight pants.

In the primordial days of cavemen and cavewomen, fashion was a matter of survival mixed with a dash of prehistoric pizzazz. Cavemen faced minimal pressure to dress provocatively, opting instead for practical loincloths that spared them unnecessary attention during mammoth hunts. Their style mantra? Comfort first, fashion maybe. Meanwhile, cavewomen navigated a more intricate fashion landscape, balancing the demands of gathering berries with the need to look fabulous in saber-tooth accessories. They bore the brunt of societal expectations, pioneering the art of stone-age chic with flair. From leopard-print loincloths to stylish shell necklaces, their wardrobes were a canvas for both expression and adaptation. These early gender norms set the stage for fashion evolution, proving that even in the dawn of time, clothing spoke volumes about identity and societal roles—albeit with fewer online reviews and more grunts of approval around the communal fire.

Next time you see a guy in a polo and khakis, remember he's not just playing it safe—he's dodging fashion grenades and navigating the battlefield of societal norms like a boss. Here's to practical pants and shirts that don't scream "Look at me!" unless it's for a promotion. Cheers to dressing for success, one sensible button-down at a time!

In conclusion, the journey from mammoth hunts to modern matrimony highlights the evolution of marriage as a strategic alliance essential for survival, economic stability, and social cohesion. While the early roots of marriage were deeply pragmatic, focusing on protection, resource management, and social status, the essence of these unions has transformed over millennia. Today, marriage still carries echoes of its ancient origins but has evolved into a partnership based on mutual respect, love, and shared aspirations. The next time you attend a wedding, remember that the ceremony is not just a celebration of love but also a nod to the intricate history of human relationships.

Chapter 5

Love in Mammoth Times: Caveman and Cavewoman Romance Tips

The 1981 movie "Caveman" is like "The Flintstones" on steroids, taking us back to a time when Tinder was just rubbing two sticks together. Atouk, our lovable caveman protagonist, is on a quest to win Lana's heart, but he's got competition from Tonda, the hulking tribe leader who probably lifts mammoths for fun. Lana digs Tonda's "robust Alpha Caveman image"—because who wouldn't want a guy who can wrestle a T-Rex barehanded?

Amidst dino-dodging and tribe politics, Atouk and his gang of misfits face challenges that make modern dating woes look like child's play. It's a hilarious peek into prehistoric life where "Netflix and chill" meant huddling around the fire and sharing a mastodon leg. "Caveman" proves that even back then, love—and laughter—were timeless pursuits, even if your pickup line was just a grunt and a club swing.

While we might not have selfies from prehistoric times, anthropologists have dug up some ancient relationship dynamics, like how the OG Native Americans did their thing. They were all about cultural know-how, like classifying a bison versus a sabertooth—critical stuff!

Enter Roger Keesing and his cognitive anthropology wisdom. He's like the Indiana Jones of culture, shifting from "How do we classify mammoths?" to "How do we classify Aunt Edna's fruitcake?" Turns out, culture's not just about totems and cave paintings; it's the mental handbook for not getting kicked out of the tribe.

Next time you're pondering prehistoric love, remember it's not about the flowers or the clubbing (well, maybe a little about the clubbing); it's about navigating the mental minefield of who's bringing home the mammoth bacon!

"Marriage: The Ultimate Cultural Rubik's Cube"

Cognitive anthropologists, those brainiacs, started by asking, "How do people group things?" Turns out, it's not just about sorting rocks and berries. They got deep into beliefs, values, and rules—basically, how to avoid getting whacked by a saber-toothed tiger or grandma's opinion on your cave art.

Then came the real kicker: organizing our lives like a cosmic Marie Kondo. From recipes for a mammoth stew to routines for clubbing (the social kind, not the mammoth-bashing kind), it's all about fitting into the tribe's mental IKEA manual. Now they're onto the big leagues: connecting culture with cognitive science. Knowing why your cavemate thinks mammoth meatloaf is a delicacy is just as crucial as dodging that flying spear. Ah, the joys of intellectual evolution!

"Men and women's relationships are like a game of tug-of-war, except both sides are pulling to see who can avoid making dinner tonight."

Ever wonder why early Native Americans tied the knot? Turns out, it wasn't just about snagging the best teepee in town. It was all about tribal alliances, making sure everyone got invited to the mammoth roast, and ensuring the gene pool stayed as deep as the Grand Canyon. And oh boy, did they have rituals! Some tribes did rain dances, others threw tomahawk bouquet tosses—anything to make Tinder look like child's play. It's like their own version of "Say Yes to the Buffalo Hide Dress."

Nowadays, we're trying to figure out the grand unified theory of marriage, blending cognitive anthropology with brain science. Because nothing says "I love you" like understanding how your significant other organizes their mental mammoth-hunting strategy. Ah, the romance!

"Men and women's relationships are like trying to fold a fitted sheet together—awkward, confusing, and guaranteed to leave you both laughing at the end."

The Native American wedding playbook: Step 1, find someone from another tribe—because variety is the spice of life, and marrying your cousin is so 1491. Step 2, no favoritism here folks! It's all about equal-opportunity marriages. We matchmake based on population sizes—like, if you're the only eligible bachelor in town, prepare to be the most popular guy at the powwow.

And let's talk rules: Tribes have them like how Anglo-Americans with the same name awkwardly shake hands. It's all about showing respect, unless you're talking to your cousin Steve from the other side of the canyon.

Forget Tinder, people; it's all about tribal connections and family ties—because in Native American households, it's not just "I do," it's "I do, and my cousin's cousin does too." Cheers to cultural customs and keeping the gene pool deep!

The original pioneers of relationship status updates: Native Americans. Back in the day, it was all about economic partnerships and keeping up with the Joneses—literally, because you might be moving in with your wife's family.

Polygamy? Totally a thing until recently, because nothing says "family bonding" like sharing a teepee with a few extra wives. And speaking of homes, the ultimate Native American relationship dilemma: whose family's place do we crash at after the wedding? No Airbnb back then!

And if things didn't work out, divorce was casual—like, "Hey, I think I left my buffalo horn comb at your place, and oh, by the way, we're done." Low divorce rates historically, but now? Let's just say, that if Facebook were around, their relationship status would be "It's complicated," thanks to modern life and too many buffalo selfies.

Ultimately, the essential qualities in relationships and bonding can vary widely depending on cultural, personal, and relational contexts. Some universally valued qualities include:

Trust: The Comedy Central of Relationships

Trust, the cornerstone of any solid relationship, is like a delicious cake made of reliability, honesty, and mutual respect. It's what keeps partners from hiding in separate caves during tough times, instead building a cozy, emotional fort where they can binge-watch mammoth-hunting documentaries together. Just remember, it takes a lot of trust to share your best mammoth-hunting secrets.

Communication: Emoji Overload

Effective communication isn't just about grunts and pointing at berries anymore. It's all about active listening (even when your partner's going on about the latest cave paintings), expressing thoughts without grunting like a mammoth, and respecting each other's opinions—even if they think saber-tooth tiger stripes are so last ice age. Mastering the art of emoji-like expressions can save you from a lot of prehistoric misunderstandings.

Respect: Boundaries and Mammoth Manners

Respect isn't just about not eating the last saber-tooth steak without asking—it's valuing beliefs, boundaries, and the sacred right to hog the fire pit. Treat each other with kindness and recognize that sometimes, a caveman needs his alone time in the cave to ponder the meaning of life.

Empathy: Feeling Mammoth-Sized Feels

Empathy is what separates the stone-hearted from the stone-cold awesome. It's about understanding your partner's struggles with giant sloth wrestling and celebrating their victories over particularly stubborn berry bushes. Connecting emotionally and offering support when the hunt doesn't go as planned—that's empathy, cave-style.

Compatibility: Finding Your Saber-Tooth Soulmate

Compatibility means more than just liking the same cave paintings. It's about sharing life goals (like finally mastering fire-making) and agreeing on whether to paint the cave walls with stick figures or something more abstract. When you both prefer cave-side sunsets to saber-tooth traffic jams, that's compatibility, baby.

Commitment: More Than Mammoth Mondays

Commitment isn't just sticking around until the first frost—it's investing in the relationship's future, even when saber-tooth catnip is tempting. It's weathering the ice ages together, prioritizing the partnership over solo mammoth hunts, and always leaving a torch lit for your cave companion.

Affection and Intimacy: From Fire Pit to Heart Pit

Affection and intimacy aren't just about physical closeness (although a warm mammoth hide hug never hurts). It's about emotional connections, like sharing a saber-tooth blanket during a cave blizzard or carving heart-shaped stick figures into tree trunks. Expressing love and appreciation, cave-style.

Conflict Resolution: No More Clubbing Each Other

Healthy conflict resolution is about mastering the art of compromise—like letting your partner hog the mammoth leg for once and negotiating whose turn it is to sharpen the spears. It's about finding a middle ground—preferably not where the woolly rhinos roam—and celebrating victory with a victory dance (preferably not involving cave-painting mud). Instead of resorting to clubbing each other, learn to talk it out, even if it means grunting in harmony.

Shared Experiences: Mammoth-Sized Memories

Shared experiences aren't just about mammoth hunts and saber-tooth skirmishes. It's about bonding over hobbies like cave painting and spear-throwing competitions, going on epic adventures to explore the other side of the mountain, and celebrating milestones like discovering fire for the first time. Make memories, one prehistoric high-five at a time, and enjoy those moments when you both finally figure out how to start a campfire without singeing your fur.

Support and Encouragement: From Rocks to Rock Stars

Supporting each other through saber-tooth scares, celebrating berry-gathering victories, and encouraging personal growth (like finally figuring out how to grind nuts for a better mammoth stew) are all part of nurturing a rock-solid relationship. It's about having each other's back, even when the cave bats are driving you batty. Be each other's biggest cheerleader, even if your pom-poms are made of leaves and twigs.

In the end, trust and the joys of cave-ship aren't just about surviving—they're about thriving, evolving, and making sure your mammoth hide is big enough for two. Cheers to love, laughter, and never forgetting to leave the cave clean for the next ice age!

Back in the day, marriages weren't just about swiping right or left on a saber-toothed tiger dating app. No, no! It was a full-on competition of "survival of the fittest." The strongest warriors got to pick their partners like they were choosing mammoth meat at a prehistoric supermarket. Forget about compatibility tests or shared hobbies—marriage was all about who could wrestle a woolly mammoth without breaking a sweat. Ladies, imagine the pressure of being chosen by the guy who could out-roar a saber-toothed cat! It's like being the prom queen of the Stone Age. Finally, next time you're complaining about your relationship drama, just remember: at least you didn't have to prove yourself by hunting down dinner with a spear!

Circumnavigating the complexities of modern relationships can feel like a prehistoric adventure, but the essentials of trust, communication, and compatibility remain timeless. From mammoth hunts to matrimony, the journey of love has evolved, yet the core values of support, empathy, and shared experiences continue to shape our bonds. So, whether you're battling saber-toothed tigers or the latest dating app, remember that building a strong relationship is about thriving together, laughing through the challenges, and creating lasting memories. Cheers to the enduring quest for love and companionship, one mammoth-sized step at a time!

Chapter 6

Caveman Communication: Grunt Decoding 101

Imagine the first couples' counseling sessions in caveman times. Caveman and Cavewoman had their own ways of saying "take out the trash" or "stop leaving mammoth bones everywhere," leading to some serious misunderstandings. When things got heated, they didn't yell or grunt louder—they reached for their stone-age language dictionaries!

Picture this: a Caveman flipping through his dictionary, a Cavewoman tapping her foot impatiently, and a prehistoric translator scratching their head trying to figure out if "ugh" means "I love you" or "get out of my cave." They might not have had smartphones, but they definitely had their ways of decoding relationship mysteries!

"Me find perfect gift for wife: Big rock. Ugh, she likes shiny things."

Back in cave times, Caveman and Cavewoman's language could be as confusing as modern-day emojis. They had words that sounded the same but meant totally different things. For Caveman, "hunting mammoth" meant "I'm providing for us," while for Cavewoman, it translated to "another night of mammoth meat stew."

When misunderstandings arose, instead of slamming cave doors, they had a novel approach: calling in a "communication mammoth," aka a translator. Imagine that scene—Caveman grunting, Cavewoman sighing, and the translator scratching their head, trying to decipher whether "grunt-grunt" meant "I'm sorry" or "go sleep with the saber-toothed tiger." In those days, trust and understanding were so critical that they'd rather hunt together than hunt each other down over a misinterpreted mammoth call!

"Ugh, me not need alarm clock. Hungry saber-tooth tiger do trick."

In today's world, translators are still in high demand, especially when it comes to decoding the mysterious language of relationships between men and women. When a woman says, "I feel like you never listen," it's not a statistical analysis of your listening habits—it's more of a heartfelt plea for attention. But men, bless their logical souls, often take it literally and start counting how many times they've zoned out during Netflix.

Women have this unique gift of using "never," "always," and "you know" like spices in a five-star recipe—liberally and with profound emotional intent. It's like saying, "You always leave the toilet seat up!" really means "Can we please have a civilized discussion about bathroom etiquette?"

In this handy guide, we decode the nuances of complaints that often get lost in translation, along with classic male responses that may need a touch of finesse and understanding. Because in the battle of the sexes, sometimes all it takes is a translator—or a really patient pet mammoth—to keep the peace!

"Women who seek to snuggle are seen as affectionate, while men who do the same are often labeled needy."

Here are some things that come out of modern social stereotypes:
- A married woman without employment is considered a homemaker, whereas a married man without a job is viewed as a failure.

- When a man expresses his opinion, he is perceived as intense and passionate, but when a woman does the same, she is often deemed bitchy and shrill.
- While a woman raising children is considered natural, a man doing so is often seen as lacking a meaningful pursuit.
- Men who enjoy zug zug   are admired and viewed as powerful, while women with the same inclination are often labeled as sluts and whores.
- A woman who cries is seen as being in touch with her feelings, but a man who cries is often regarded as weak. A woman who gets angry is irrational. A man who gets angry knows and gets what he wants.

A man skilled in the art of straightforward communication, focusing solely on facts and figures, might find himself in a linguistic labyrinth when trying to decode a woman's emotional map. When a woman declares, "I don't feel heard," he might nod, thinking he's aced the listening test because he can parrot back her exact words. Little does he know, it's like navigating through a cave with Google Maps—close, but missing all the hidden emotional pitfalls.

Women speak in emotional hieroglyphics, where "I don't feel heard" is less about auditory prowess and more about telepathic connection. It's the emotional equivalent of saying, "The Wi-Fi signal between us is weaker than my last diet attempt." Men, however, equipped with their trusty literal translation guide, might respond with a logical flowchart outlining the times they did listen (or at least looked like they did).

To truly grasp the ancient art of understanding women's feelings, gentlemen, think less like a caveman deciphering cave paintings and more like a psychic Tarzan swinging through emotional vines. Because in the jungle of relationships, the right translation can mean the difference between a cozy campfire and a saber-toothed tiger chase.

"Oh, it's like my words are doing the mammoth mambo and you're over there doing the saber-tooth shuffle!" "Can you sprinkle a little interest seasoning on my word salad, please?"

If a man can decode her complaint accurately, he'll dodge more arguments and earn bonus points for emotional acrobatics. It's like cracking the Enigma code but with more feelings and fewer submarines. When misunderstandings hit, it's like watching two species trying to communicate with Google Translate—there are bound to be some hilarious lost-in-translation moments.

Picture this: She says, "I'm fine," and he hears, "All systems go." But in reality, it's DEFCON 1, and he's about to walk into an emotional minefield. Or when she mentions "nothing," it's really "something," and it takes a PhD in emotional intelligence to figure it out. Missteps are inevitable, like accidentally sending a message in emojis that says "I love spaghetti" instead of "I understand your feelings."

Navigating these conversations can feel like walking a tightrope while juggling flaming torches. One wrong move, and you're in the doghouse. But get it right, and you're the hero of the day, dodging arguments with the grace of an Olympic gymnast and racking up points like you're playing emotional pinball. Gentlemen, grab your decoder rings and get ready for the most rewarding challenge of your life—because figuring out what she really means is like finding the Holy Grail, but with fewer knights and more date nights.

"Show me you're not just nodding like a bobblehead mammoth; give me the full caveman eyebrow raise of understanding!"

Men sometimes miss the memo that women speak in feelings, not just facts. Therefore, when she says, "I feel like you never listen," it's not a multiple-choice quiz where repeating her words verbatim scores an A+. It's more like deciphering a riddle wrapped in an enigma wrapped in emotional saran wrap.

Imagine she's speaking in Morse code, but your translator is stuck in emoji mode. She says, "I feel like you never listen," and you respond with, "I hear you." Congrats, you just missed the deeper message that requires a bit more emotional sleuthing. What she's really saying might be, "I need more attention and understanding," and figuring that out is like solving a Rubik's Cube blindfolded.

It's all about tuning into the emotional frequencies. When she drops hints, like "I'm cold," it's not just about temperature; it's about craving warmth and comfort, both physically and emotionally. Or when she mentions, "We never go out anymore," it's not a mere observation—it's a call for more shared experiences and quality time.

Guys, think of it as a spy mission: you need to decode her feelings with precision and care. You're not just aiming to defuse a bomb—you're aiming to understand the intricate wiring of her emotions. Every nod, every "I see," and every empathetic gesture is a step closer to mastering this art.

Remember, it's less about providing solutions and more about offering genuine empathy. When she vents about a bad day, she doesn't need you to fix the problem with a PowerPoint presentation; she needs a comforting presence, a "that sounds really tough" hug, and maybe some ice cream.

Gentleman, embrace your inner Sherlock Holmes and decode those feelings with finesse. It's not just about avoiding the doghouse; it's about building a fortress of trust, understanding, and emotional intimacy. After all, in the grand game of love, speaking her language is the ultimate power-up.

But back in Caveman times, they had it sorted. They probably had an ancient Rosetta Stone for emotions—none of this grunting and hoping for the best. They understood that "I don't feel heard" isn't a code for "Your hearing test results are in," but more like, "Your emotional Wi-Fi needs a reboot."

Modern men, when you find yourself in a verbal battle over what she really meant, channel your inner Caveman wisdom. Embrace the nuances, dodge the misunderstandings, and remember: decoding emotions is like navigating a Jurassic Park full of friendly T-rexes.

The Caveman Calendar: From Full Moons to Mammoth Hunts!

When a Cavewoman says, "We never go out," it's not a scathing review of his social planning skills—it's more like a gentle nudge towards a candlelit dinner. In Cavewoman language, "never" often translates to "H ey, let's spice things up, how about some quality time?" It's like deciphering hieroglyphs: "We never go out" actually means "I'd love a date night, and I'd love it even more if you took charge and made it happen."

But if a caveman hears it as "You're a hopeless couch potato," well, that's a classic lost-in-translation moment. Instead of catching the romantic hint, he might miss the memo entirely and start defending his Netflix skills, boasting about his binge-watching prowess. Meanwhile, she's sitting there, hoping he'll get off the couch and make dinner reservations, wondering how her subtle hint turned into a debate about the merits of TV marathons.

"Me have Hunting day and resting day"

My fellow cavemen, when you decode her hints like an ancient Rosetta Stone, you're not just preventing an argument—you're unlocking the secret level where she feels understood and cherished. It's like becoming an honorary Caveman, fluent in emotional nuances and ready to conquer the next date night quest.

When a Cavewoman says, "Everyone ignores me," it's not just a simple statement—it's a full-on emotional map. In Cavewoman language, it's like saying, "Hey, I'm feeling a bit invisible right now. Your work's been getting a lot of attention, and I'm over here waving like a T-Rex in the brush. I know you're busy and all, but a little acknowledgment would go a long way."

But if a Caveman hears it as "You're neglecting me for your job," well, that's like reading hieroglyphs upside down. He might think she's accusing him of being a workaholic when really, she's just asking for a bit of spotlight time.

Cavemen, when she drops hints in ancient language like "Everyone ignores me," it's not a cave critique—it's a call for a little attention and appreciation. Translate it right, and you'll win her heart faster than you can say "mammoth steak dinner."

Cavewoman: "I want to forget everything." Caveman (translation): "Me hunt mammoth alone. You sit cave, do nothing."

Cavewoman: "I am so tired, I can't do anything."

Caveman (translation): "Me think you lazy. Me need strong cavewoman, not sleep all day."

Cavewoman: "Could you please embrace me and express how cherished I am in your eyes?"

Caveman (translation): "Me hear: you weak. Me no understand 'cherished'. Me find mammoth, you feel cherished."

Cavewoman: "I am overwhelmed."

Caveman (translation): "Me hear: me fail as caveman. Me need better plan to make cave peaceful."

Cavewoman: "I want to talk about our feelings."

Caveman (translation): "Me hear: me need learn many grunts. You say more, me understand."

Cavewoman: "Choosing you was a mistake."

Caveman (translation): "Me hear: you think other caveman better. Me need prove strong, catch big fish."

Cavewoman: "I want to be alone."

Caveman (translation): "Me hear: me annoy. Me find more mammoth alone."

Cavewoman: "I need some time to myself."

Caveman (translation): "Me hear: me need improve cave paintings. You happy then."

Cavewoman: "I'm not sure where our relationship is going."

Caveman (translation): "Me hear: me need find bigger cave. You want bigger cave."

Cavewoman: "I just need you to listen."

Caveman (translation): "Me hear: me not listen before. Me listen now." Cavewoman: "I want us to grow together."

Caveman (translation): "Me hear: me not good enough. Me get better, grow big like tree."

Cavewoman: "I want more romance."

Caveman (translation): "Me hear: me no good at flowers. Me pick more flowers."

Cavewoman: "I want to feel appreciated."

Caveman (translation): "Me hear: me not say 'good hunt' enough. Me say more."

Cavewoman: "I need you to be more supportive."

Caveman (translation): "Me hear: me not strong enough. Me lift bigger rocks."

Cavewoman: "I want to resolve our conflicts."

Caveman (translation): "Me hear: me hit rock, you hit rock. We talk after."

Cavewoman: "I love you."

Caveman (translation): "Me hear: me love you too. Me catch mammoth for us."

When a Cavewoman says, "This house is always a mess," it's like she's carving a message in stone: "Hey, today I'm feeling tired, and this cave looks like a herd of woolly mammoths stampeded through it. I could really use a hand. Could you maybe pitch in and help clean up a bit?"

But if a Caveman hears it as "You're a slob," well, that's a bit like mistaking a cave painting of a bison for a squirrel. He might think she's criticizing his tidiness skills when all she really wants is a helping hand. Cavemen, when she drops ancient hints like "This house is always a mess," it's not a prehistoric slam—it's a gentle nudge for teamwork. Decode it right, and you'll avoid a cave-dwelling catastrophe faster than you can say "rock scrubbing."

When a caveman hears, "This house is always a mess," it's like decoding an ancient cave painting gone wrong: "You, sir, are a disaster! Your mess-making skills rival those of a rampaging saber-toothed tiger. Clean up or risk extinction from this cave!" Clearly, his interpretation might need a bit of evolutionary fine-tuning. Instead of seeing it as a prehistoric ultimatum, maybe he should consider it more like a friendly reminder to pick up a broom and sweep his way back into her good graces. On the contrary, when a caveman says "This house is always a mess," he's basically asking to be clubbed with a mammoth-sized broom.

Cavemen and Cavewomen communication styles can clash like rocks and mammoth tusks! When Cavewomen speak their minds, it's like they're narrating their entire thought process out loud—no cave is left unexplored! Meanwhile, Cavemen are more like ancient philosophers pondering life's mysteries silently in their cave corner.

When Cavewomen are wondering why their Caveman is as quiet as a sleeping saber-toothed tiger, maybe it's just because he's brewing up the perfect response, like a stone-aged artisan crafting the perfect spear. It's a clash of communication styles that's been happening since the dawn of time—just with fewer emojis and more grunts!

"Ugh, me no need Wi-Fi. Me have real friends fire."

Women have been cracking the code of men's silence since the Stone Age, wondering if it's a signal of doom or just a caveman contemplating the meaning of life. When a man goes quiet, it's like he's vanished into a prehistoric cave, leaving a trail of anxious thoughts in his partner's mind: "Is he plotting my demise with a dinosaur?" "Did he forget I exist?" or "Maybe he's just inventing fire in his head."

For women, a man's silence isn't always golden; it's more like a mystery box filled with worst-case scenarios. When in doubt, grab a torch and explore that cave of silence carefully—it might just be where he's storing all the unspoken feelings and leftover mammoth meat!

"Ugh me hunt food. Wife hunt for best cave decorations."

When one woman listens to another, it's like a verbal dance where "uh-huh," "hmmm," and "ah" are the supportive moves that keep the conversation grooving. It's a reassuring rhythm that says, "I'm with you, sister!" But when a man enters the conversation, his silence can feel like a sudden blackout during a dance-off—it's unnerving!

For women, decoding a man's silence is like deciphering ancient hieroglyphs. Does his quiet mean he's contemplating the meaning of life or just pondering what's for dinner? By embracing his need for solitude, women might uncover the hidden treasures of his thoughts and respond with a supportive "uh-huh" or a knowing "hmmm" when he finally emerges from the caveman cave of silence.

"Me make fire. Fire good. Fire warm. Fire not good for eyebrows."

Ah, the mysterious cave of the Caveman! When a man retreats into his cave, it's like a secret bunker where he hides from life's trivialities—like deciding what to eat for dinner or figuring out where the TV remote vanished. For Cavewomen, this is a test of patience akin to waiting for a sloth to finish a marathon. Should they disturb the tranquility of the cave? Should they bring offerings of mammoth meat and soothing grunts?

But fear not, dear Cavewomen! Remember, entering the cave uninvited is like crashing a party in the Stone Age. Your Caveman needs his space to wrestle with the mysteries of the universe (or just figure out how to fix that leaky mammoth bladder). Ladies resist the urge to rescue him from the depths of his man cave. Let him emerge when he's ready, with newfound wisdom on why saber-tooth tigers avoid broccoli. In the end, it's all about understanding the ancient art of Cavemanology—a delicate dance between support and solitude, mammoth meat and peaceful grunts, and the occasional well-timed   "U   h-huh."

"Who need wheel? Feet already come with free parking!"

Ah, the perplexing dynamics of the Caveman-Cavewoman emotional dance! Cavewomen, armed with their sharpened instincts and ready to dive deep into the labyrinth of emotions, often find themselves lost in a maze of misunderstandings. They wield their arsenal of questions like spears, hoping to pierce through the veil of silence and uncover the hidden treasures of their Caveman's thoughts.

But alas, what they perceive as an act of heroic empathy can sometimes feel like a relentless barrage of interrogations to the poor Caveman. Imagine being cornered by a curious pterodactyl asking, "How do you feel about that? What's on your mind? Why did you say 'hmm' instead of 'ah'?"

It's enough to make even the most stalwart Caveman retreat deeper into his cave!

In this ancient saga of relationship evolution, both parties must learn the delicate art of emotional navigation. Instead of wielding their emotional compasses with reckless abandon, Cavewomen should trade inquisitiveness for understanding—realizing that sometimes, the way to a Caveman's heart is through silent companionship and a well-timed grunt of solidarity.

Because let's face it, decoding the caveman code requires a blend of intuition, empathy, and knowing when to lay off the questions and enjoy the mammoth roast together.

"Cave sweet cave, where the walls have more echoes than my ex!"

Ah, the saga of the man's cave—a rocky refuge where men retreat to brood over life's mysteries and the occasional sock left on the floor. Picture this: a rugged Caveman, seeking solace amidst his cave paintings after an epic battle with the woolly mammoth of workplace woes. His Cavewoman, armed with a spear of good intentions and a hide-bound quest for resolution, ventures forth.

But alas! The Cavewoman, in her valiant attempt to unravel the mystery of the brooding Caveman, stumbles into a prehistoric pickle. Unaware that his grunts and huffs are not invitations to a fireside chat, she plunges headlong into conversation. "Hey, what's bugging you, my boulder-hearted beau? Let's talk it out," she implores, wielding her emotional toolkit like a seasoned saber-tooth tamer.

Yet, as she delves deeper into the rocky recesses of his cave, she uncovers not the pearls of emotional revelation she sought, but the echoing abyss of misunderstood intentions. For the caveman, this intrusion is like a saber-toothed tiger crashing his post-hunt nap—it disrupts his primal need for solitary contemplation. He feels cornered and confused, wondering why his quiet time has suddenly turned into an emotional expedition he never signed up for.

"Me no need map. Me follow the sun, then realize I've been going in circles around the same rock!"

In this comedic caveman drama, the moral is crystal-clear: sometimes, the best way to support a Caveman isn't with words, but with the unspoken language of understanding and a respectful retreat to let his ancient grumbles settle like sediment in a prehistoric pond. After all, in the wild world of relationships, mastering the art of "cave diplomacy" can be the difference between a saber-toothed success and a mammoth-sized misunderstanding!

Ah, the enigmatic "I am OK" in Caveman-speak—a linguistic puzzle wrapped in a fur loincloth. Picture this: a stalwart Caveman, facing the perilous task of taming a saber-toothed spreadsheet at the office cave. His Cavewoman, armed with the wisdom of their phrase dictionary, deciphers his gruff declaration.

"Cavewomen bitch at me, complain I know nothing."

But lo and behold! Little does she know, "I am OK" isn't just a statement—it's a saga. A saga of stoic self-sufficiency, of mammoth-sized independence. It's Caveman shorthand for "I've got this, darling. No need to worry your lovely prehistoric mind. Trust in my ability to wrestle this mammoth of a problem solo."

Yet, in her noble quest to decode his cryptic cave talk, the Cavewoman plunges headlong into the thorny thicket of misunderstanding. Armed with her arsenal of questions and concern, she unleashes a torrent of well-meaning queries.

"Are you sure you're OK? Is there anything I can do? Maybe we should talk about it?"

Alas, her earnest attempts to decode his condensed communication fall flat. For the Caveman, her well-intentioned inquiries sound like the mating call of a pterodactyl—loud, confusing, and distinctly unhelpful in his quest for solitary mammoth taming.

In this rib-tickling caveman comedy, the lesson is clear: sometimes, when a Caveman says, "I am OK," it's not just a statement—it's a prehistoric haiku of self-assurance. And the best way for a Cavewoman to support him? Perhaps a knowing nod, a reassuring pat on the back, and a solemn vow to leave the saber-toothed spreadsheet to its solitary fate. After all, in the rocky terrain of relationships, understanding the art of "Cavemanese" can be the difference between a woolly mammoth of success and a dodo of misunderstanding!

Ah, the delicate dance of marital communication—a waltz through the wilds of emotional expression and domestic diplomacy. Picture this: a weary writer, hunched over his keyboard, crafting literary masterpieces and fending off deadlines like a digital gladiator. Enter the spouse, a valiant navigator of household affairs, armed with queries and concerns.

In this riveting scene from the domestic drama "Eternal Tales of Matrimony," our protagonist, the intrepid writer, is thrust into the arena of relational rhetoric. His spouse, with the finesse of a seasoned negotiator, probes the progress of his latest literary conquest. "I'm nearing completion," he valiantly declares, eyes bloodshot from battling with words and wrestling with deadlines. Yet, just as victory seems within reach, a tempest of emotional exchange looms on the horizon.

"Ugh, Rock-paper-scissor? Me think rock always win."

Cue the poignant soliloquy from his spouse, a symphony of overwhelmed sighs and lamentations on the scarcity of quality time. In the past, our gallant writer might have brandished the sword of defensiveness, listing every moment of shared bliss or extolling the virtues of deadline sanctity. Alas, such tactical errors only fueled the flames of marital skirmish, transforming their humble abode into a battleground of miscommunication.

But fear not, dear reader, for enlightenment awaits! Our hero, having survived many a verbal joust, unveils the secret to marital harmony: understanding, empathy, and the strategic deployment of attentive listening. No longer does he wield the shield of rebuttal; instead, he dons the cloak of comprehension, ready to navigate the labyrinthine corridors of emotional discourse.

"Ugh, me need food, games, zug zug; she need thing to hang on cave walls, meat in back of cave, no zug zug, she angry now"

And so, in this epic tale of love and literature, the moral is clear: when the spouse cometh with grievances, heed not the call of defense, but embrace the art of empathetic engagement. For in the kingdom of matrimony, victory lies not in rebuttal, but in the gentle symphony of shared understanding and the occasional, begrudging acknowledgment of laundry day procrastination. Thus concludes our chapter from "Eternal Tales of Matrimony," where love, laughter, and the occasional snarky comment reign supreme.

Steering the intricate language of relationships might seem daunting, but learning to decode those emotional cues can transform misunderstandings into meaningful connections. Embracing the nuances of communication and showing genuine empathy isn't just about avoiding conflict—it's about building a stronger, more intimate bond. Thus, take a cue from our prehistoric ancestors: listen, understand, and appreciate each other's unique ways of expressing love and needs. In the end, it's all about turning those grunts and sighs into shared laughter and lasting companionship.

Chapter 7

Desire Decoded: Caveman 'Zug Zug' Insights

Imagine the whispers in ancient caves: men, as cavemen, always chasing mammoths, ready to club anything that moves, while cavewomen need the moon in the right position and berries just so. The lore goes that men's sharp spears are fueled by mammoth juice, always hunting and grunting. "Men's zug zug fire ignites quickly, like striking a rock," while "women's zug zug fire needs a complex dance of stars and cave paintings."

But new research etchings tell a different story. Everyone has a fire inside; some just need more kindling, maybe a good joke or shiny rock. The idea that men are perpetually ready to chase mammoths and women need a cave painting oversimplifies things. New studies show that zug zug drive cannot be neatly divided into "male" or "female." Men's zug zug drive is like a fast mammoth chase—ready to sprint at the sight of a hoof and always eager. Women's zug zug drive is more like a cave painting expedition—taking time to decipher the symbols, but once connected, it's a leisurely journey full of story-telling and communal grunting.

The notion that men are always ready to chase mammoths and that women need perfect cave conditions is outdated. Dr. Justin Grog from the Kinsey Institute at Rockville College explains it's about societal norms dictating that men should be vocal about their mammoth interests while women remain quiet.

Social norms influence how people talk about their mammoth-hunting experiences, hunting buddies, and even mammoth pictures. In one study, college students were divided into three groups: those who knew their answers would be public, those hooked up to a fake lie detector, and those who just told their stories straight. The mammoth tales varied based on who was listening—details like the number of mammoth wrestles or mammoth painting viewings changed with the audience.

Men's zug zug drive is often compared to a bottomless mammoth feast—always ready for more. Women's zug zug drives are more like a cave chef's special—savoring each bite, critiquing the seasoning, and wondering if more mammoth spice is needed. When hooked up to the fake lie detector, men reported fewer mammoth-hunting buddies, while women's mammoth-cozy nights increased. The mammoth tales got a bit more adventurous with the phony lie detector.

According to research, men reported an average of 3.7 sexual partners, and women reported 2.6 when they thought peers would see their answers. However, when told their answers would be anonymous, men reported 4.4 partners, and women reported 4.0. "Men's zug zug drives are like a firecracker—quick, explosive, and done. Women's zug zug drives are like a slow-burning candle—steady, warm, and lasting."

Not all men are constantly roaring like cave bears in heat. About 1 in 6 cave dudes face low sexual desire due to stress, relationship issues, and daily mammoth hunting chores. Hunter Murray reminds us, "Men aren't just cave robots programmed for non-stop mammoth chasing."

Determining who's got the bigger mammoth-hunting urge is like counting stars on a cloudy night. Direct questions don't always yield clear answers. About half of college-age couples were on the same mammoth-hunting wavelength. When desires clashed, half the time it was the guy not feeling the mammoth mojo. Hunter Murray confirms that men can be just as likely as women to want a break from the chase.

"Men's zug zug drives are like a TV with too many channels—constantly scanning for something exciting. Women's zug zug drives are like a favorite book—they appreciate the buildup, character development, and emotional connection."

Hunter Murray's research shows that men's and women's mammoth-chasing desires are more alike than different. However, for transgender and nonbinary cavefolk, the research is still emerging. Murray emphasizes that sex drive and gender are not strictly defined—some cavefolk are more mammoth-hungry than others, and that's totally normal if it leads to happy mammoth-hunting.

"Men's zug zug drives are like a light switch—easily turned on and off. Women's zug zug drives are more like a dimmer switch—adjustable, nuanced, and responsive to the right atmosphere."

The zug zug drive is like comparing mammoth-hunting strategies: some are always ready to charge, while others prefer to negotiate mammoth treaties. If we're wondering who's more likely to chase mammoths, we might consider how often cave ladies sharpen their spears, what kinds of mammoth herds they prefer, and if they're into solo mammoth tracking or group hunts.

"Men's zug zug drives are like a superhero—always ready to spring into action. Women's zug zug drives are like a secret agent—strategically planning the mission and ensuring everything aligns perfectly."

Someone with a high desire for mammoths will think about them more than someone just curious about the occasional saber-toothed cat. Eysenck (1971) found that men think about mammoths more than cave ladies. Researchers Laumann, Gagnon, Michael, and Michaels (1994) found that men's thoughts about mammoths outnumbered women's.

Men often think, "Every day, let's hunt mammoths!" while women are more like, "Maybe next moon phase." Beck, Bozman, and Qualtrough (1991) confirmed it: men are more frequent mammoth chasers, while some cave ladies debate their need for a new mammoth   skin rug.

"Men's zug zug drives are like a microwave—quick and straightforward. Women's zug zug drives are like a slow cooker—taking time to simmer and blend flavors."

Jones and Barlow (1990) tracked young adults' mammoth-chasing urges for a month. Men reported nearly five mammoth urges a day, while women reported just a couple. Men's mammoth fantasies were off the charts! It seems mammoth hunting and daydreams vary greatly among cavefolk.

Tracking arousal is like following mammoth footprints—men's arousal is as clear as a trail, while women's is more elusive. Nutter and Condron (1983) found that women with less mammoth mojo had fewer mammoth hunt fantasies. Leitenberg and Henning (1995) found men dream of mammoths more often, with more variety in their fantasies.

Measuring the zug zug drive is like counting mammoth bones: those really into mammoth hunting are willing to trade a lot to satisfy their desire. Historically, cave dudes with more resources could splurge on mammoth taming tools. Today, everyone has access to mammoth traps, but men still tend to spend more on mammoth pictures and entertainment than women.

In a nutshell, the stories about mammoth-hunting urges aren't so cut and dry. Studies show men's and women's mammoth-chasing desires are more alike than different. However, the research on transgender and nonbinary cavefolk is still emerging. Understanding sex drive and gender is complex, but recognizing the variety in mammoth desires is crucial for happy mammoth-hunting!

Chapter 8

From Cave Paintings to Hormones: The Truth About 'Zug Zug'

O ur ancient cave scribbles and modern studies often depict the late 1900s and contemporary societies. Back then, Western cave dudes were all about daily mammoth hunts, while cave ladies preferred a more relaxed schedule. The real question is whether these ancient desires are hardwired in our genes or just part of societal trends.

In ancient times, the division of labor between men and women was primarily driven by the necessities of survival. Men, with their greater physical strength and endurance, typically took on the roles of hunters, venturing out to pursue large game like mammoths. Their days were filled with the physical demands of tracking, hunting, and hauling back their catches. This relentless pursuit of food required them to develop skills in coordination, strategy, and endurance. The success of the hunt was crucial for the survival of the tribe, and men's roles were vital in ensuring a steady supply of meat, hides, and other resources.

Meanwhile, cavewomen managed the home front, gathering edible plants, caring for children, and maintaining the living spaces. This role was equally essential, as it ensured the tribe had a stable and safe environment. Women developed a keen knowledge of their local environment, understanding which plants were edible, which had medicinal properties, and how to avoid dangerous flora and fauna. They also built strong social networks within the tribe, sharing knowledge, resources, and support. This division of labor was a practical adaptation to the challenges of prehistoric life, optimizing the strengths and abilities of each gender for the benefit of the community.

Fast forward to the late 1900s and contemporary societies, and we see a significant shift in these roles. Industrialization, technological advancements, and societal changes have transformed the way we live and work. The traditional roles of men and women have evolved, with both genders participating more equally in various aspects of life. Men are no longer solely responsible for providing food and protection, and women are not confined to domestic tasks. The lines have blurred, with both men and women pursuing careers, hobbies, and lifestyles that suit their individual preferences and aspirations.

Modern studies and societal observations often explore whether these ancient roles are deeply ingrained in our genetic makeup or simply a result of long-standing societal norms. Some researchers argue that certain behaviors and preferences are indeed hardwired, a product of evolutionary pressures that shaped our ancestors' lives. For instance, the drive for men to seek out physically demanding tasks and women to excel in nurturing and social roles might have roots in our prehistoric past.

However, others contend that societal trends and cultural expectations play a significant role in shaping our behaviors. The late 1900s, for instance, saw a dramatic shift in gender roles, with women entering the workforce in unprecedented numbers and challenging traditional norms. This period highlighted the impact of social change and the ability of individuals to adapt and redefine their roles. The feminist movements of the 20th century further catalyzed these changes, advocating for gender equality and dismantling stereotypes that had persisted for centuries.

Today, the balance between nature and nurture continues to be a topic of debate. Are our preferences and behaviors a result of genetic predisposition, or are they molded by the society we live in? The answer likely lies in a complex interplay of both factors. While our evolutionary past has undoubtedly influenced certain aspects of our behavior, the dynamic nature of human societies means that cultural and societal trends also play a crucial role in shaping who we are.

In modern times, the pursuit of careers, hobbies, and lifestyles is increasingly influenced by personal choice rather than rigid societal expectations. Men and women are redefining their roles based on their interests, strengths, and aspirations, breaking free from the constraints of traditional norms. This evolution reflects the adaptability and resilience of human beings, demonstrating our capacity to shape our own destinies while acknowledging the influences of both our genetic heritage and the societal structures we inhabit. As we continue to navigate the complexities of modern life, understanding this balance between nature and nurture remains key to fostering a more inclusive and equitable society.

In caveman times, genetics played out like a dramatic series: Caveman genes focused on "hunt, gather, procreate," while Cavewoman genes emphasized finding a protective and resourceful mate. This prehistoric saga of survival and romance intertwined mammoth-sized desires with cave art dreams.

However, our ancient genetic blueprint isn't the complete picture of our mammoth-sized activities. Hormones are the true influencers, like the cave version of "Keeping Up with the Mammoth Hunters." They tweak our desires, ensuring we're aligned with our instincts, whether hunting mammoths or sketching them on cave walls.

On a serious note, testosterone is a key hormone distinguishing males from females. Men generally have much higher levels—around 1,000 nanograms per deciliter compared to women's 100-150 nanograms per deciliter, as experts like Dabbs (2000) and Mazur & Booth (1998) note. Postmenopausal women often have significantly lower testosterone levels.

Picture Caveman trying to impress Cavewoman with his fire-starting skills, only to be met with a headache-induced rejection due to her rock-gathering project. This scenario humorously highlights the dynamic between their different desires and daily activities.

"Genetics wired Cavemen to pursue mates with the stamina of a mammoth hunt, and Cavewomen to seek partners who can multitask—hunting, gathering, and still remember to pick up cave milk."

Other theories about mammoth-sized desires are like competing cave paintings. Levine emphasizes biological mammoth signals, suggesting our drives are urgent needs, while Singer and Toates argue our brains act like command centers, firing signals for mammoth pursuits akin to hunger pangs.

Social scientists propose that mammoth desires are both personal and communal. This dynamic shows how our individual goals are intertwined with social bonds, much like deciding whether to chase mammoths alone or with a buddy. Essentially, our urge to chase mammoths is deeply connected to how much we value and love our cave mates, blending personal ambition with communal affection.

"In this cave soap opera of mammoth desires, everyone's got a theory, and the mammoth hunt continues!"

Biological models of mammoth-sized desires involve ongoing debates, especially regarding hormones like testosterone and estrogen. Researchers suggest testosterone ignites mammoth hunts in cave dudes but that isn't the whole story. Bancroft (1988) even hints that spontaneous cave drawings (sexual urges) during sleep might reveal deep-rooted cravings, contrasting with dreams or visual stimuli.

For women, it's a maze of hormones—estrogen keeps things smooth, progesterone throws curveballs, and testosterone affects hunt frequencies and responses. In this hormonal saga, each hormone plays a role, stirring up cave drama.

Testosterone and estrogen are like a dynamic duo, each adding flair to sexual chemistry. For men, testosterone boosts libido, ensures erections, and flexes muscles. For women, estrogen manages puberty, menstrual cycles, and lubrication. Together, they create a hormone-fueled symphony of desire and satisfaction, proving that behind every great performance, there's a balanced hormonal cast ensuring everything goes smoothly.

Alexander and Sherwin (1993) found that higher testosterone levels in oral contraceptive users didn't necessarily increase mammoth painting interest. Schreiner-Engel et al. (1989) found no clear hormonal clues to women's mammoth desires. It's like trying to read mammoth tracks in the dark—full of surprises, with hormones playing hide-and-seek.

The Economics of Zug Zug: Intimacy as Currency

Sexuality in modern cave society is like trading mammoth tusks— sometimes about love, sometimes about securing attention or future benefits. Some cave ladies genuinely enjoy the mammoth chase, but often, it's more about deal-making than cuddles. If there were mammoth dealings before marriage, who kept track of the ledger? It's like counting mammoth prints in the snow—confusing and not straightforward.

Viewing zug zug as an exchange within marriage—trading intimacy for affection, favors, or material goods—adds a transactional layer. This perspective treats intimacy as a marital currency, potentially eroding its spontaneous and affectionate nature. Over time, this dynamic can strain the relationship, making genuine emotional and physical closeness harder to achieve.

Now, let's address the mammoth in the cave: Does the trade-off of mammoth pleasures play a role in your marriage foundation? Are you both aware of the mammoth deals happening? Addressing these dynamics can strengthen your partnership, both emotionally and physically. It's time to face the cave truth for a satisfying life inside and outside the bedroom.

In some marriages, zug zug can become a tactical tool for control, like using mammoth snacks as leverage. This dynamic distorts healthy relationship dynamics, turning intimacy into a power play. The affected partner may feel objectified and emotionally isolated, while the controlling partner misses out on genuine emotional benefits.

Men often fall for sex as a quid pro quo due to deep-rooted desires and the allure of intimacy, leading them to agree to various demands in hopes of gaining sexual favor. This dynamic can turn the bedroom into a battlefield for control, leaving men feeling manipulated and women like guilty puppeteers.

For a relationship to thrive, couples need to recognize and address the misuse of zug zug as a power tool. Open communication and understanding each other's perspectives are essential. Establishing boundaries and agreements can ensure both partners feel valued and respected. Professional help from therapists or counselors can also provide a neutral ground for exploring these dynamics.

Alternatively, zug zug can deepen emotional and physical intimacy when approached with mutual enthusiasm and care. This shared experience builds trust, reinforces emotional ties, and provides a unique form of communication. By seeing zug zug as a way to connect deeply, partners can foster a more fulfilling relationship.

Mutual Consent and Respect: The Ideal Expression of Intimacy

Ideally, zug zug in a healthy marriage is based on mutual consent, respect, and a desire to connect intimately. It should be a natural expression of love and affection, not a commodity to be traded. Prioritizing each other's comfort and pleasure strengthens the relationship's foundation, encouraging open communication and creating a safe space for genuine intimacy.

Zug Zug Insights: The Caveman vs. Cavewoman Perspectives

Men's perceptions of zug zug often harken back to caveman days, driven by primal urges and societal expectations of sexual prowess. Stereotypes suggest men can easily detach emotions from sex, seeking multiple partners to leave a genetic mark. Dominance and control in the bedroom reflect ancient needs to prove worth. Despite these stereotypes, every man's viewpoint on sex is unique.

Meanwhile, women's perspectives are a dance between biological urges and societal pressures. Biologically, women seek emotional intimacy and connection, looking for partners who provide security and support. Society reinforces that sex should be deeply emotional, valuing quality over quantity. Individual beliefs vary, influenced by everything from rom-coms to family advice.

For cave couples, it's about respecting each other's boundaries and prioritizing mutual satisfaction, communication, and emotional connection. Like keeping the cave fire burning—warm and cozy, with occasional sparks in all the right directions. A cave without communication is like a mammoth hunt without a plan—confusing and full of surprises!

Caveman and the truth about Zug Zug

Men need sex for a variety of reasons, some of which are more compelling than others. On a biological level, testosterone, the primary male sex hormone, is like a tiny coach constantly yelling, "Go team!" and pushing for reproduction, ensuring the survival of the species.

Emotionally, sex can be a way for men to connect with their partners, fostering intimacy, strengthening relationships, and proving that they can multitask better than just holding a remote. Plus, engaging in sexual activity can help reduce stress and release endorphins, leading to feelings of happiness and well-being—kind of like a gym session but without the sweaty gym clothes. Regular sex is also associated with various health benefits, such as improved heart health and immune function, so it's practically a workout routine, just way more fun. For many men, sexual activity can boost self-esteem and confidence, affirming their desirability and attractiveness, which is a nice bonus when you're trying to rock those dad jeans. Societal norms and cultural expectations often emphasize the importance of sexual prowess and activity in defining masculinity, influencing men's attitudes towards sex and their perceived need for it, because nothing says "manly" like attempting to interpret complex emotional signals while simultaneously remembering where you left the car keys. Beyond reproduction, sex is a source of physical pleasure and enjoyment—a reminder that while life can be a grind, it doesn't always have to be. The pursuit of pleasure is a fundamental aspect of human behavior, and sex is a natural and enjoyable way to achieve it. These factors can vary widely among individuals, and not all men may place the same importance on sex or experience the same drives, but let's face it, who's going to turn down a chance to combine cardio with cuddling?

Cavewomen and the truth about Zug Zug

Women need sex for a variety of reasons that span the same reason why Cavemen need it; biological, psychological, and social domains. Biologically, sex plays a role in reproductive health and hormonal balance, with oxytocin, the "love hormone," fostering emotional bonding and intimacy, making connections deeper without the need for endless heart-to-hearts. Psychologically, sex offers pleasure, stress relief, and improved mood thanks to endorphins—nature's way of saying, "You deserve a cookie, but better." Physically, it brings benefits like improved cardiovascular health, a boosted immune system, and better sleep, making it the ultimate multitasking workout. It also enhances self-esteem and body image, affirming attractiveness and desirability. Socially, cultural norms and personal experiences shape attitudes towards sex, making it more fun than yoga and far less awkward than small talk at networking events. Overall, sexual satisfaction is linked to well-being and quality of life, making it an important aspect for many women. And if it means swapping a night of Netflix for a different kind of "chill," who's really complaining?

Ultimately, the Truth About 'Zug Zug,'" is about the evolution of human desires from the ancient scribbles on cave walls to contemporary scientific studies, questioning whether our behaviors are hardwired in our genes or shaped by societal trends. Historically, the division of labor between men and women was driven by survival needs, with men hunting mammoths and women gathering plants and caring for children. Today, industrialization and societal changes have blurred these traditional roles, allowing for greater equality and personal choice in careers and lifestyles. The interplay between nature and nurture is complex, with both genetic heritage and cultural expectations influencing our behaviors. Hormones like testosterone and estrogen play significant roles in driving sexual urges and shaping interactions. Moreover, viewing intimacy as a transactional exchange within relationships can strain genuine connections, highlighting the importance of open communication and mutual respect. Ultimately, understanding the balance between our evolutionary past and societal influences is key to fostering deeper, more fulfilling relationships in modern life.

Chapter 9

The Sensitive Caveman: A Deep Dive into Feelings

U nderstanding the differences in sensitivity between men and women is like trying to navigate a mammoth herd in a cave with only a flickering torch—it's complex, confusing, and sometimes you stumble upon unexpected mammoth droppings. Biological, psychological, and cultural factors all play a role in shaping how we handle mammoth-sized emotions and thoughts. On a biological level, hormones like testosterone and estrogen influence how men and women respond to emotional stimuli, affecting their sensitivity to stress, empathy, and emotional regulation. Psychologically, differences in brain structure and function can lead to variations in how men and women process emotions and social cues.

Culturally, societal norms and expectations have historically shaped the ways men and women express sensitivity and handle emotional situations. In the cave era, men were often expected to be stoic hunters, channeling their sensitivity into physical endurance and aggression, while women were encouraged to be nurturing and attentive to social nuances. These roles, though ancient, still echo in today's expectations and behaviors, influencing how individuals of each gender perceive and express sensitivity.

Sure, we can make some generalizations—like how cave guys might roar louder during mammoth hunts, while cave ladies might spot those elusive mammoth details—but cave individuals are as unique as mammoth tusks. Sensitivity isn't just about feeling mammoth emotions; it's also about how we navigate cave relationships and even the occasional cave workplace drama. Recognizing and appreciating these differences can lead to better communication and understanding, fostering more harmonious and supportive relationships both in the cave and in modern life.

"Men have two feelings: happy and mad"

while

"Women's feelings are a whole emotional symphony"

Folks, whether you're a caveman with a sensitive side or a cave lady with mammoth-sized resilience, remember: sensitivity isn't a one-size-fits-all mammoth pelt. It's a wild cave journey filled with surprises and the occasional mammoth-sized laugh echoing through the cave walls.

Hormonal Circus and Mammoth Brain Battles

Biologically speaking, it's like comparing mammoth tusks to cave paintings: men with their testosterone bravado and risk-taking tendencies might charge headfirst into emotional caves, while women, bathed in estrogen's glow, are like cave detectives sniffing out every emotional mammoth print. It's a hormonal circus where one side roars and the other side reads mammoth minds!

And let's not forget our cave brains—like comparing a mammoth's tusk to a cave club. Women's amygdalas, those emotional hotspots, are like fireworks on mammoth hunt night, while men's brains light up with thoughts of mammoth strategy and cave conquests. It's a neurological dance where emotions collide with mammoth-sized logic, leaving cave couples scratching their heads over who moved the mammoth hide!

Mammoth Mind Games: Navigating the Cave of Mixed Messages

Psychologically speaking, it's like navigating a cave full of mixed messages and mammoth-sized expectations. From the get-go, cave boys are told to toughen up and chase mammoths, while cave girls are handed mammoth-hugging lessons and told to watch out for emotional mammoth traps. It's like trying to tame a mammoth with a feather—boys learning to be stoic while girls navigate a minefield of nurturing and empathy, all while trying to avoid mammoth-sized emotional mishaps.

And let's talk about emotional regulation—like comparing mammoth snacks to cave painting tools. Women, with their social support-seeking strategies, are like cave networkers, weaving emotional webs around the cavefire. Meanwhile, men sharpen their mammoth-hunting skills, focusing on practical solutions while occasionally missing the emotional mammoth tracks right under their noses. It's a cave drama where mammoth-sized emotions meet practical cave logic, leaving everyone wondering who's got the mammoth-sized emotional toolkit!

Cave Culture Chaos: Mammoth Sensitivity and Stoic Hunts

Sociocultural factors are like navigating a mammoth migration through a cave—some caves encourage emotional mammoth trumpeting for everyone, while others restrict it to cave ladies only, with occasional "no feelings allowed" signs for cave guys. It's a cultural jamboree where sensitivity levels swing from mammoth-hugging communal caves to stoic mammoth-hunting grounds, leaving cave psychologists scratching their heads over who's got the right mammoth attitude.

And don't even get started on cave workplaces! Women, with their cave networking prowess and emotional radar, are like mammoth whisperers leading teams through emotional cave mazes. Meanwhile, men sharpen their mammoth-hunting skills, laser-focused on cave goals and assertiveness, leaving everyone else wondering if they accidentally stumbled into a mammoth negotiation or a cave team-building exercise. It's a professional jungle where sensitivity meets mammoth-sized ambition, with occasional cave misunderstandings along the way!

Mammoth GPS: Navigating Sensitivity and Cave Stereotypes

Understanding sensitivity differences between men and women is like trying to navigate a mammoth migration with a cave GPS—sometimes it leads you right to the mammoth cave, and other times you end up in a cave painting class. Recognizing individual variations is key because cave folks aren't just mammoth chasers or cave painters; they're a complex mix of emotional mammoth enthusiasts and practical cave decorators. It's like trying to find the right mammoth emoji in a cave full of mixed signals and emotional mammoth traps!

And let's talk about challenging gender stereotypes—it's like trying to teach a mammoth to mambo in a cave disco. Education and awareness about sensitivity differences are crucial because cave norms can be as confusing as a mammoth with a paintbrush. We're all in this mammoth migration together, from cave biologists studying mammoth emotions to cave decorators picking the right emotional cave decor. Embracing sensitivity diversity means we all get to enjoy the mammoth-sized party of understanding and respect, with occasional cave misunderstandings adding spice to the mammoth stew!

In conclusion, navigating the complexities of sensitivity between men and women is much like steering through a mammoth herd with only a flickering torch—an endeavor filled with confusion, unexpected turns, and the occasional mammoth dropping. This intricate dance of emotions is influenced by biological, psychological, and cultural factors that shape how each gender processes and expresses feelings. From the primal days of cavemen and cavewomen, where roles were defined by survival needs, to modern times where societal norms continue to evolve, the ways we handle emotions have been deeply rooted in both our genetic makeup and societal expectations.

Understanding these differences is crucial for fostering better communication and empathy, whether in personal relationships or the workplace. Men might roar louder and focus on practical solutions, while women often navigate emotional nuances with finesse, but ultimately, each individual is as unique as a mammoth's tusk. By appreciating these differences and challenging stereotypes, we can create a more inclusive and understanding environment, ensuring that the journey of sensitivity is navigated with respect and mutual support. Whether you're a caveman with a sensitive side or a cavewoman with mammoth-sized resilience, recognizing and valuing each other's emotional landscapes can lead to more harmonious and fulfilling connections, proving that sensitivity, like a mammoth hunt, requires teamwork and understanding.

Chapter 10

Mammoth Hunt: Surviving Long-Term Love

Long-term relationships are like taming a saber-toothed tiger: one moment, you're cuddling it like a pet, and the next, you're running for your life. Cavemen and Cavewomen understand this well—discovering the perfect mammoth-hunting spot only to find it's haunted by mammoth ghosts. One day your partner is sharing mammoth tales around the fire, and the next, they're throwing mammoth bones at you in a heated argument. This is the cave drama that keeps mammoth psychologists busy!

You've probably seen it in your cave too—your partner goes from offering you the biggest mammoth steak to giving you the cold shoulder. It's enough to make you wonder if cavemen invented emotional roller coasters! Just when you think you've mastered cave love, bam! It's like trying to build a fire with wet mammoth fur. Love's unpredictability turns cave romances into a daily survival game where trust and mammoth-sized emotions collide!

Ah, the roller coaster of love! One moment, you're writing love sonnets on the cave walls, and the next, you're hiding behind mammoth bones to avoid your partner's wrath. It's like discovering a cave painting masterpiece, only to realize it's a Rorschach test revealing your deepest fears—like whether your partner's mammoth-hunting skills will ever improve!

Self-love is crucial, but sometimes it feels like our repressed emotions are taking the cave stagecoach straight to Crazytown. You wake up overflowing with love, only to realize you've also been hoarding resentment like a squirrel storing nuts for winter. It's like finding out your favorite mammoth fur blanket has hidden thorns—cozy until it pricks you!

And oh boy, don't get me started on the divorce thoughts! One minute you're planning a romantic mammoth barbecue, and the next you're drafting mammoth-sized divorce papers. It's like planning a cave-warming party and then realizing your cave's foundation might be built on quicksand. Can love survive when your partner's jokes feel as funny as a mammoth with a cold?

Navigating emotions in a relationship is like exploring a cave with a torch that occasionally flickers out just when you think you've found the treasure. We all carry emotional baggage—think of it as dragging a mammoth bone collection behind you. When love shines its torch on these hidden bones, suddenly you're tripping over ancient arguments and childhood fears faster than you can say "mammoth stew."

One day you're the epitome of patience and understanding, the next you're more demanding than a saber-toothed tiger at dinner time. It's like being a cave painter with mood swings—today you're creating masterpieces, tomorrow you're scribbling angry stick figures. And don't get me started on commitment-induced blindness! Once your partner says "I do," suddenly everyone with a better mammoth-hunting technique looks like a potential mate.

Repressed emotions don't come with warning labels. They sneak up on you like a surprise attack from a woolly rhino in mating season. Childhood wounds? Check. Abandonment issues? Double check. It's like discovering your cave has a secret room filled with emotional skeletons just waiting to jump out and scare the mammoth fur off you. Love may open the door to these buried feelings, but whether they bring a bouquet of flowers or a club depends on how well you've tidied up your emotional cave.

Navigating the minefield of relationship emotions is like trying to build a fire with wet mammoth dung—messy, unpredictable, and occasionally explosive. Your partner brings you flowers, and suddenly you're remembering that time they forgot your birthday faster than you can say "prehistoric amnesia." Being generous with love one moment and withholding it the next is like trying to tame a wild dinosaur—sometimes you're cuddling it, other times you're running for your life from its sharp teeth and bad breath.

When it comes to the gender divide in emotional reactions, men retreating to their caves when past mistakes come up is like trying to hide from a woolly mammoth in a kiddie pool—it's not fooling anyone. Meanwhile, women diving deep into their emotions when their past is mentioned is like exploring a cave with too many twists and turns—you never know when you'll stumble upon a hidden treasure chest or a sleeping bear.

Remembering the 90/10 principle in these heated moments is like trying to cook with only half the ingredients—sometimes it works, and sometimes you're left with a burnt saber-toothed tiger steak. In the heat of an emotional battle, suggesting your partner write you a Love Letter before unleashing their feelings is like giving them a spear before facing down a mastodon—it might not make them any less angry, but at least they won't be throwing rocks at you. And if their emotions feel like trying to wrestle a mammoth into submission, remember to give them space to calm down—it's hard to discuss feelings when you're being chased by a stampeding emotional mammoth.

When you're initially attracted to your partner, it's like discovering fire—exciting, warm, and captivating. But suddenly feeling indifferent in their presence is like realizing fire isn't great for roasting mammoth steaks—just a bunch of hot air. Feeling positive about yourself and your life can shift to feelings of unworthiness faster than you can say "caveman's club." It's like thinking you've mastered the art of making stone tools, only to realize your tools are as blunt as a prehistoric razor.

Writing Love Letters and delving into your emotions is like trying to decipher cave paintings—you might uncover the true meaning behind the stick figures or just end up with a bunch of scratched rocks. Embracing the enchantment of love and understanding underlying factors sounds nice, but it's like trying to domesticate a wild saber-tooth—cute until it tries to eat your pet mammoth. Just as negative emotions can overwhelm us, they can be swiftly released, like accidentally setting fire to the wrong cave wall.

Feeling confident in your partner's love is like thinking you've tamed a wild mammoth—until it decides to trample your garden and eat all your berries. Wanting intimacy with your partner can quickly turn into feelings of desperation and neediness, like realizing your favorite mammoth skin is covered in saber-tooth tiger bites. When your desires don't align with your partner's, it's like trying to catch a fish with your bare hands—sometimes you get lucky, other times you just end up wet and hungry.

When your partner decides to make a positive change, the other might react like a caveman who just discovered fire—initially intrigued but quickly wondering if it's worth the effort. Take Bill and Mary, for instance. When Bill finally decided to fulfill Mary's requests, she greeted him with the warmth of a frozen mammoth carcass, muttering "It's too late" or "So what." It's like trying to roast a saber-tooth steak for dinner and getting a lukewarm response from your cave buddy.

From a bystander's point of view, it's fascinating to observe couples who have been together longer than some civilizations. Imagine children growing up, mammoths going extinct, and then, out of nowhere, the wife starts eyeing the cave exit. The husband, jolted awake by the impending dino-sized asteroid of divorce, decides it's time to change. But when he finally starts showing the love she's been craving for what feels like epochs, she responds with a glare icier than a Neanderthal's morning swim. It's as if she's been storing up her resentment like a stash of flint for twenty winters, just waiting for him to make the first move. Interestingly, it can happen the other way around, too.

Picture a man ready to bolt from the cave, and the woman, seeing her favorite cave paintings threatened, finally says she's willing to redecorate. But he digs in like a stubborn mammoth in quicksand, refusing to budge. It's like he's guarding the last stash of nuts in winter, unwilling to share even when the ice age is over.

In conclusion, surviving long-term love is akin to taming an Apex Predator—one moment you're cuddling it like a pet, and the next, you're running for your life. The unpredictable dynamics of relationships keep us on our toes, reminiscent of cavemen navigating mammoth herds. Emotions in a long-term relationship can shift as dramatically as the seasons in the prehistoric era. One day, you're sharing mammoth tales by the fire, and the next, you're throwing mammoth bones in heated arguments. This constant ebb and flow of emotions requires patience, understanding, and a willingness to navigate through both the highs and lows together. It's about recognizing the complexities of our biological, psychological, and cultural influences and using that understanding to foster deeper connections. Just as cavemen relied on each other for survival, we must rely on communication, empathy, and mutual respect to sustain long-term love. Embracing the adventure of love with all its unpredictability and challenges is what ultimately strengthens the bond, making it resilient enough to withstand the test of time.

Chapter 11

Cave Art to Romance: Passion in the Stone Age

C omedies about cavemen and "zug zug"often depict men as primal creatures, stumbling over rocks and grunting in pursuit of their next romantic conquest—usually a cavegirl who's just not that into them. But how accurate are these portrayals? What really drives men's desire, and where does love fit into their quest for passion? You might think men are wired to be visually stimulated, like cave artists mesmerized by a well-drawn bison on a cave wall. Meanwhile, women are portrayed as more emotionally driven, like cave philosophers pondering the meaning of life while their mates chase after mammoths. However, modern research challenges these stone-age stereotypes.

Not everyone is a slave to their desires, regardless of gender. Some cavemen and cave ladies might prefer a quiet evening by the fire with a good rock to cuddle rather than getting tangled in the complexities of modern mating rituals. And when they do feel the urge, it's not always about the visuals. Sometimes, it's the emotional connection that lights their torches, leading to deep conversations about the cave paintings of life and love.

Recent studies have revealed that when it comes to responding to sexual and erotic images, the brain's reactions aren't strictly about which gender you were assigned at birth. In other words, men's brains don't automatically light up like a cave torch more than women's when it's time to get all hot and bothered. It turns out, exposure to saucy stuff can get all kinds of brain regions tingling in both sexes. But here's the kicker: fellas actually show less brain action and physical fireworks with each rerun of the naughty stuff, hinting that their caveman cravings might seek variety, like a new rock painting or a fresh mammoth hunt.

Men are known for their robust collection of sexy thoughts and fantasies, often being whisked away by the breeze (wink, wink). They've got a knack for wanting "zug zug" more often, having a good ol' solo session in the cave, and being the first to whip out the old mating dance moves compared to the ladies. According to relationship expert Helen Fisher, romantic relationships can be described in three stages:

1. **Lust**: Driven by physical sexual gratification and casual "zug zug".
2. **Attraction**: Attention shifts to a specific partner, focusing on spending time together.
3. **Attachment**: Bonds form with increased levels of oxytocin and vasopressin, providing comfort and security.

In the wild world of brain chemistry and romance, it's like a hormone-fueled rollercoaster ride where testosterone and estrogen are the giddy fuel for lust, sending us cavemen and cave ladies chasing each other like prehistoric Tinder matches. Then, just when things are heating up, dopamine and norepinephrine swoop in like Cupid's little helpers, showering us with pleasure and rewards. Finally, oxytocin and vasopressin come in to calm the whole cave down and make sure we stick together long enough to binge-watch the stone-age sunset.

And here's the kicker: men and women ride this hormonal rodeo equally! There's no gender-exclusive VIP section in this love carnival. Dr. Nicole Prause, the psychologist and brain maestro, even points out that despite society trying to keep love and "zug zug" in separate caves, the truth is, folks find their romps way more satisfying when there's a sprinkle of love in the mix. While everyone tries to fit love and "zug zug" into neat little boxes, our brains are like, "Nah, let's mix it up and have a party!"

Zug Zug to Cavewomen: It's Not Just About Love

For cavewomen, "zug zug" isn't just about love; it's about getting stuff done without having to ask twice! Men often think women are just as ravenous for physical satisfaction as they are. While testosterone revs up both sexes, men's libido is like a roaring bonfire, while hers is more like a quiet, simmering pot of mammoth stew. For her, it's all about the mental game—daydreams, flashbacks, and fantasies—especially when she's deep in the throes of a new crush or maybe just a really good cave painting.

According to the wise words of sex researcher Meredith Chivers, being desired is like hitting the jackpot for women. Sure, catching sight of a rugged caveman might stir some excitement, but it's his reaction to her that really lights her torch. Knowing he's into her sets off a mental fireworks display of sexy thoughts and scenarios. Women crave ongoing romance as proof they're still rocking that saber-tooth tiger pelt.

Many women enjoy "zug zug", but sometimes desire takes a rain check due to everyday stressors—like avoiding saber-tooth tiger attacks or dealing with general cave chaos. Unlike men driven by primal urges, women have these pesky "brakes" that slow things down—chores, offspring, work drama, you name it. They might approach intimacy with good intentions, but they're not always primed for action until the stars align. And let's not forget, achieving a satisfying climax can feel like trying to start a fire with wet sticks.

For women, the sexual journey often begins within the safe confines of a relationship—not in some solitary exploration like our caveman counterparts. Physical intimacy opens the floodgates of vulnerability, longing for connection, and the occasional back rub. Relationship dynamics can mess with desire levels as women seek emotional safety nets. Romance and seduction provide the perfect backdrop for shedding daily stress and focusing on what really matters—like where to find the juiciest mammoth ribs.

Zug Zug as a Component of Love

Love for women is like a multitasking mammoth hunt—zug zug is just one arrow in the quiver. It's about communication, shared responsibilities, and finding time for cave cuddles. While getting busy can definitely fan the flames of relational warmth, it's not always the blazing center of her emotional universe.

Sometimes, ladies give in to their partner's needs for a romp in the bear fur, even when they're not feeling it at first. It's an act of love, really. And don't get it twisted—many women find joy in connecting intimately, even if they're not summiting Mount Pleasure Peak every time. Sometimes, getting physical can bridge emotional gaps, even when they start off as distant as separate caves.

Ultimately, men and women both crave deep emotional bonds in their relationships, but they often come at it from different angles. Emotional and sexual intimacy together create the recipe for a love that's as enduring as a well-preserved cave painting. Men might prioritize physical closeness to feel connected, while women often seek emotional security before diving into the physical realm. Despite these differences, when both partners find a balance, it leads to a harmonious and lasting relationship that stands the test of time.

A Humorous Look at Men's and Women's Differences in Zug Zug

Men and women are like apples and mammoth steaks when it comes to the bedroom. Men, with their testosterone-driven desires, are like hormonal tornadoes. Their desire for zug zug is like an ancient fire that never goes out—thanks, testosterone, for turning them into perpetual cave studs.

Cavewomen, on the other hand, navigate a more complex hormonal landscape. Estrogen and progesterone act as cosmic choreographers of their desire dance, signaling when they want emotional closeness or just a cuddle. These hormonal fluctuations, especially during menstrual cycles, can create unpredictability, making it hard to distinguish between a yearning for love or just a natural hot flash.

Understanding these primal disparities is crucial for navigating the prehistoric dance of love and lust. Sure, men might be all "Let's go hunt some fun," while women are like, "Can we talk about our feelings first?" But when both sides get the cave memo and respect each other's wild urges and tender moments, it's like discovering fire together—warm, satisfying, and a whole lot less hairy. Here's to embracing our caveman and cavewoman roots because, in the end, we're all just trying to avoid being eaten by saber-tooth tigers and find a cozy cave to call home.

Lastly, navigating the realm of romance and passion from the Stone Age to modern times reveals that while our primal urges have evolved, the essence of love and desire remains deeply rooted in our biology and cultural norms. The comical portrayals of cavemen stumbling through romantic conquests may oversimplify the complexities of human intimacy, yet they underscore the universal quest for connection. Men and women, influenced by their unique hormonal landscapes, approach relationships with different perspectives, balancing physical desires with emotional needs. Modern research challenges outdated stereotypes, showing that both genders experience a rich tapestry of erotic and emotional responses. Ultimately, understanding and appreciating these differences, while embracing our shared humanity, allows us to foster deeper, more fulfilling relationships. From the flickering torch light of cave paintings to the bright glow of contemporary love, the journey of romance is a testament to our enduring need for connection and intimacy.

Chapter 12

Grunts to Greatness: Caveman Chat Skills

Women speak Cavemanese with a flair for superlatives, descriptions, and generalizations. Meanwhile, Cavemen are often as clueless as a mammoth in a snowstorm when it comes to decoding these messages. They take everything literally, inevitably leading to responses that sound more like grunts than support. Here are some classic examples of how Cavemen might unintentionally drop the boulder when responding to Cavewomen's not-so-subtle hints:

Cavewoman: "I'm so tired today." **Caveman's response**: "Okay." **Caveman's thoughts**: Is that good? Bad? Did she mean, 'I'll take care of everything'? Or maybe 'Okay, don't expect me to do anything'? Should I just grunt?

Cavewoman: "Do you think she's prettier than me?" **Caveman's response**: "Um, I guess." **Caveman's thoughts**: Oh no, danger ahead! Should I say no? But then I'll sound like I'm not paying attention. Yes? But what if she gets mad at me for lying? Um, guess it is!

Cavewoman: "Could you help me with the chores today?" **Caveman's response**: "Later." **Caveman's thoughts**: Later? But when is later? Later today, later this moon, later this age? I better go find that mammoth first.

Cavemen's responses to Cavewomen's statements often land squarely in the land of "facts and figures," aiming to swiftly end the conversation like a well-thrown spear. Little do they know, their Cavewomen are looking for more than just stone-cold facts; they're seeking connection, empathy, and maybe a hint of understanding. In the ancient dance of communication, Cavemen might be mentally sifting through rocks trying to unearth the right response, while the true answer lurks silently in their cave of thoughts. This mismatch in communication styles leads to more misunderstandings than a failed attempt at fire-starting.

This linguistic chasm is the source of many a rock-wielding argument and echoes of frustration bouncing off cave walls. Cavewomen often lament, "I don't feel heard," a grievance as old as the saber-toothed tiger. Cavemen scratch their heads, wondering if grunting louder might suffice. Even Cavemen, creatures of the hunt and gather, struggle to decode this perennial complaint. After all, deciphering what Cavewomen truly desire as a response is as tricky as trying to domesticate a wild mammoth.

Cavewoman: "Are you listening to me?" **Caveman's response**: "Yes, of course." **Caveman's thoughts**: "I really don't care! But I know this is a trick question, 'yes' is always the safest answer."

It's like navigating through a woolly mammoth stampede. When a Caveman hears, "I don't feel heard," he might respond by trying to solve the problem or defending himself, thinking he's nailed the issue. To really get through to him, a Cavewoman should rephrase it like this: "I don't feel heard." Of course, the Caveman might still miss the mark, prompting her to add, "Could you at least pretend to care about my thoughts?" If the guy got the point, he'd argue less and nod more enthusiastically. When Cavemen and Cavewomen hit argument mode, it's usually because they're speaking different dialects, like two rival cave clans. It's crucial to translate or rephrase what they've heard before the saber-toothed misunderstandings escalate!

Cavewoman: "How do I look in this outfit?" **Caveman's response**: "You look fine." **Caveman's thoughts**: "I am so tired of falling into this trap. Fine is the safest word in the jungle!"

Cavewomen often use dramatic language and vague hints, expecting their Cavemen to decode the hidden requests within. While other Cavewomen understand this indirect style, Cavemen are left scratching their heads, oblivious to the hidden agenda. If Cavemen could just crack the code and respond appropriately, they might avoid being banished to the cave for the night!

Cavewoman: "What are you thinking?" **Caveman's response**: "I have work on my mind." **Caveman's thoughts**: "Stop talking, I just want to chill and not think about anything!" **Cavewoman**: "Hello, mammoth in the room! Can we please focus on what matters here?"

One of the biggest hurdles for Cavemen is deciphering and genuinely backing a Cavewoman when she vocalizes her feelings. Conversely, Cavewomen's primary challenge lies in grappling with the silence of a Caveman, which often feels like navigating through a dense jungle blindfolded. When a Caveman suddenly shuts down and goes quiet, it's akin to a rare solar eclipse in the Cavewoman community—unheard of and baffling. Initially, a Cavewoman might interpret this silence as a sign that the Caveman isn't listening, assuming his lack of response means he's mentally off on a mammoth hunt instead of tuning into her emotional terrain.

Cavewoman: "Is the car okay to drive to LA; are you sure?" **Caveman's response**: "Yes, it's fine to drive." **Caveman's thoughts**: "OMG, for the 10th time, there is nothing wrong with the car! She's treating it like a saber-toothed tiger on wheels."

Cavemen and Cavewomen process information differently, leading to communication breakdowns and arguments. Cavewomen tend to think out loud, sharing their inner discovery process with an attentive listener. This confuses Cavemen because they assume Cavewomen want a response when, in reality, they don't. Often, a Cavewoman finds clarity on what she wants to say simply by talking it through. It's like she's brainstorming out loud while Cavemen are left trying to decode her stream of consciousness. This free-flowing of thoughts helps Cavewomen tap into their instincts, which is like watching them hunt for clarity in the wilds of everyday conversation.

Cavewoman: "I do not like your friend; why do you still talk to him?" **Caveman's response**: "I know; he is that one friend." **Caveman's thoughts**: "I don't care; I have to live vicariously through him now that I am married."

In contrast, Cavemen process information more internally. Before uttering a single word, they meticulously analyze the received information. They ponder over the best possible response, sometimes taking minutes, hours, or even a few epochs of geological time. If a Caveman requires more information to formulate a response, he might opt for silence, leaving Cavewomen to ponder whether he's contemplating the mysteries of the universe or just zoned out thinking about dinosaur football.

Cavewoman: "Why do you act like such a baby when you get sick?" **Caveman's response**: "I know." **Caveman's thoughts**: "Because you nag me even when I'm sick! Can't a caveman just have some peace and quiet?"

Women often jump to wild conclusions when men stay silent, depending on how they're feeling that day. She might start cooking up scenarios like, "He never listens to me," "He doesn't give a caveman's grunt about my feelings," or "He's off in his man cave, ignoring me again."

This can spark an argument that she'll keep fanning until her Caveman surrenders his independence.

When a Caveman clams up, it's like a neon sign flashing "Danger!" in a Cavewoman's mind. Typically, Cavewomen go silent only when what they have to say could start a volcanic eruption or when they've lost faith in someone and are dodging interaction. Cavewomen get jittery when a Caveman goes all quiet!

Cavemen retreat into their silent caves when Cavewomen start sentences with "Why," "How come," "You don't," "You need to," or the dreaded "I don't feel." Cavemen aren't wired to catch every thought bubble that pops into your head. They might miss the hints, but that doesn't mean Cavemen are heartless.

Most men tend to be straightforward in their thoughts and actions. They often do not overanalyze their actions or rehearse their words before speaking. Many men act and speak spontaneously, without necessarily harboring positive or negative intentions behind their words or deeds. However, societal norms and gender stereotypes often lead to a simplistic view of all men through a singular lens.

The concept of 'he said, she heard' is all too familiar. Often, when a man genuinely tries to help or be friendly towards a woman, his actions are misinterpreted by some of the opposite gender. There is an assumption that his intentions must be driven by ulterior motives, even when that's not true. It's like a guy holding the door open for a woman and she's like, "Oh, he's definitely plotting something." Or when he offers to carry her heavy bags and she's thinking, "What's his angle? Is he trying to impress me or just show off his muscles?" It's tough being a guy sometimes; you're just trying to be nice, and suddenly you're a suspect in the court of female perception.

Cavewoman: "You are embarrassing me!" **Caveman's response**: "I am sorry." **Caveman's thoughts**: "No, I'm not; I don't care what your friends or their husbands think. In fact, I'm just warming up for my next performance!"

It's a conundrum for women to grasp that a man can be nice without any hidden agenda. There's always that lingering doubt: why else would he be nice? Maybe he's just genuinely sweet and polite to everyone? When a man gives a compliment, it's often mistaken for flirting. And if he goes out of his way to help, it's automatically assumed he's plotting something. But hey, sometimes a good deed is just a good deed, no strings attached!

Frequently, when a woman interrupts a man, no one bats an eye. But when the roles reverse, suddenly it's like the guy just kicked a puppy in front of everyone. And if a man dares to suggest she lower her voice, well, he might as well be defusing a bomb while riding a unicycle—it's that dramatic! All he wants is a chance to make sense, not start a Shakespearean tragedy.

Cavewoman: "I want to have a baby." **Caveman's response**: "That would be great." **Caveman's thoughts**: "Sweet! More zug zug for me, baby!"

The line between chivalry and chauvinism is about as clear as a cave painting in a sandstorm. Take this: I offer to help her carry mammoth bones back to our cave, and suddenly I'm accused of thinking she can't handle it because she's a woman. It's not about thinking she's weak; it's about showing off my hunting skills and hoping she notices how strong I am. I mean, who wouldn't want a partner who can wrestle a saber-toothed tiger, right?

Caveman Perspective

You see, when I offer to help her carry a mammoth-sized suitcase or figure out those confusing tax rocks, it's not because I think she can't handle it. It's because I've got these impressive biceps and want to show them off—like, check out my hunting muscles, right? But then she gives me that look like I'm some sort of ancient sexist. Hey, I'm just trying to be helpful and impress her at the same time. Can a guy not multitask?

Cavewoman Perspective

It's like, he's offering to carry my stuff, and I appreciate the gesture, but does he think I'm some helpless cave-lady? I mean, I can wrestle a saber-toothed tiger if I have to! And the mansplaining? He'll explain how to sharpen a spear like I've never held one. Honey, I've been spearing fish since before we had wheels. It's cute he wants to share, but sometimes I just need him to listen and not act like he invented fire.

Ah, mansplaining—like explaining to her how to tie a knot when she's been weaving baskets since we were kids. Picture this: I'm passionately explaining how to sharpen a spear, and she's nodding like she's already the tribe's expert on weapons. Sometimes, I just want to share my wisdom, you know? It's not that I think she doesn't know stuff; it's just that I think I know stuff better. But hey, as long as she's not aiming a spear at me, I think we're good.

Men and emotions—a saga more epic than the hunt for the elusive giant sloth. If I shed a tear watching a cave painting of a sunset, suddenly I'm a "sensitive soul," but if I show no emotion when a bear charges at us, suddenly I'm "too tough for feelings." It's like trying to catch a woolly mammoth with a broken spear—frustrating and confusing. If I bottle it up, I'm like a stone slab; if I let it out, I'm like a waterfall during the monsoon season. Can't a caveman just feel without being judged?

Fellas, let's embrace our emotions like we embrace a freshly caught fish—fully and without worrying about what the other cavepeople think. And ladies, maybe cut us some slack; sometimes our emotions are as unpredictable as a stampede of mastodons. We're just trying to navigate this prehistoric world the best way we know how, okay? This can be problematic for several reasons:

Spear-Making 101: Thanks, But I've Got This

Imagine you're the top spear-maker in the tribe, and some caveman insists on explaining the finer points of flint knapping to you. It's like, "Excuse me, I've been crafting weapons longer than you've been chasing antelopes!" Next thing you know, he's asking if you need a cave-dwelling manual. Oh please, spare me.

Herbology for Dummies: Caveman Edition

There I am, trying to explain the nuances of gathering herbs for healing when Mr. Know-It-All steps in to explain the medicinal properties of roots I've known since birth. Sure, because clearly, I need a caveman to enlighten me on my own herbal remedies. Thanks, but no thanks, I'll stick to curing ailments without the unsolicited herbology lessons.

Basket Weaving with a Side of Stereotypes

You know, when some caveman starts mansplaining how to weave a basket, it's not just irritating—it's like he's trying to turn back the Stone Age clock. Like, dude, just because I'm weaving doesn't mean I can't figure out the best vines for the job. Let's not perpetuate the stereotype that women can't weave without a caveman's step-by-step guide.

Caveman Communication: Less Lecturing, More Listening

Here's a thought: if cavemen spent less time asserting their opinions and more time listening, maybe we could actually exchange ideas without me having to assert my dominance over who knows more about tracking game. It's not a contest, okay? Just a friendly conversation... without the caveman lecture series.

Confidence Crushers: The Flint Axe of Mansplaining

Nothing boosts my confidence like a caveman implying I don't know the difference between a saber-tooth and a sloth. Seriously, when you constantly get mansplained about the simplest things, it's like they're trying to chip away at my self-esteem with a flint axe. Guess what, buddy? I've got this, and your unsolicited wisdom isn't helping.

Ah, yes, the infamous mansplaining—a surefire way to turn a casual conversation into a full-blown lava eruption. It's like being handed a torch and told, "Let me show you how fireworks," while you're the one who discovered it in the first place. Mansplaining isn't just a nuisance; it's like trying to teach a saber-toothed cat to fetch—unnecessary and likely to get you clawed.

Women don't get mad about mansplaining because they secretly enjoy a condescending lecture. No, it's more like watching a caveman try to explain the wheel when you're the one who invented the axle. It's as if every caveman who mansplains thinks he's unraveling the mysteries of fire, forgetting that you're the one who built the first bonfire!

Mansplaining doesn't just trigger eye rolls; it's like being told how to use a spear by someone who still misses the mammoth every time. It's like arguing with a rock—no matter how much you explain, it just doesn't get the point. Next time a caveman feels the urge to mansplain, maybe he should try inventing something new—like silence! Here are some reasons why:

Firestarter Faux Pas: Discounted Knowledge at the Stone Age Marketplace

You know, it's like having someone explain how to start a fire with two sticks when you've already lit up half the village. Mansplaining makes me feel like my brain's on sale at the Stone Age marketplace: "Discounted knowledge, just because she's a woman!"

Spear-Splaining: Thanks, But I Know My Mammoth

Imagine hunting mammoths for years, only to have a caveman explain that I'm holding the spear wrong. Thanks for the input, but I think I've got a handle on this, buddy. It's not just about the spear; it's about respecting my years of mammoth-hunting expertise!

Wheel Wonders: Keeping Stone Age Stereotypes Alive

When a caveman explains why a wheel works, it's like he's trying to convince me we need a cavewoman version with flowers painted on it. Oh, because wheels are too advanced for us, right? Thanks for keeping the Stone Age stereotypes alive.

Grain Grinding Gripes: Let's Skip to the Bread, Please

You see, when a caveman insists on explaining how to grind grain, it's not helpful—it's like he thinks I've been grinding air for the last decade.

How about we skip the grind and get to the bread already? I've got cave mouths to feed.

Cave Art Critique: Undermining Confidence with Charcoal Commentary

Nothing boosts my confidence like a caveman explaining why my cave paintings could use more "saber-tooth realism." Yeah, because nothing says confidence like being critiqued on my artistic flair by a guy who can barely draw a straight line with charcoal.

Finally, to promote respectful and equitable communication, the caveman should listen actively, value their cavewoman's perspectives, and avoid assuming her knowledge based on their gender. It's like navigating a dense jungle: sometimes you need to trust her map rather than insist on carving your own path with a stick.

Of course, on the flip side is "Womensplaining," a phenomenon as common as a saber-toothed tiger sighting in a cave. Womensplaining occurs when a woman explains something to a man in a tone that suggests he just discovered fire for the first time. It's like trying to explain the benefits of fire to someone who's still struggling to rub two sticks together without setting their loincloth on fire. Just as cavemen should avoid treating cavewomen like they've never seen a wheel; cavewomen might want to skip the lectures on mammoth hunting techniques to someone who's been at it since the Stone Age. Womensplaining can create several problems in communication and relationships just as mansplaining does, for example:

Cave-splaining Woes: Reinforcing Gender Myths

Just like "mansplaining," Womensplaining can reinforce stereotypes about gender roles and knowledge. It's like assuming every guy can't figure out how to operate a club without a woman's detailed instructions. Imagine a cavewoman telling her caveman how to properly arrange stones for a fire, as if he hasn't mastered the art of making sparks since he was a young Neanderthal.

Mammoth Miscommunication: When Explaining Goes Too Far

Just like Mansplaining, when women engage in Womensplaining, it can lead to a breakdown in meaningful communication. It's like trying to discuss the migration patterns of woolly mammoths while one person is busy explaining the basics of cave painting techniques to the other. Instead of swapping insights and building on each other's knowledge, it becomes a contest of who can out-explain whom.

In this scenario, the original topic of conversation gets lost as one person dominates the dialogue, focusing on details that might be unnecessary or already understood. The dynamic shifts from a mutual exchange of ideas to a one-sided lecture, leaving the other person feeling patronized and unheard. This can be particularly frustrating when both parties have valuable insights to share but are unable to do so due to the imbalanced conversation.

Such interactions can stifle collaboration and innovation. Instead of working together to solve a problem or share expertise, the conversation becomes a power struggle. The person being Womensplained to might feel their intelligence and contributions are being undermined, leading to frustration and disengagement. They may start to withdraw from the conversation, feeling that their perspective is not valued or respected.

Moreover, this dynamic can create an environment where open communication is discouraged. If one partner consistently feels overshadowed or belittled by the other's constant explaining, they might become hesitant to share their thoughts and ideas in the future. This can lead to a communication gap, where important insights and solutions are overlooked because one person feels it's not worth the effort to speak up.

To prevent Womensplaining, and Mansplaining, from derailing meaningful communication, it's important for both partners to practice active listening and mutual respect. Acknowledging each other's expertise and contributions fosters a more balanced and collaborative conversation. By focusing on listening as much as explaining, partners can ensure that their discussions remain productive and respectful, allowing for a true exchange of ideas and insights.

Cave Cold Wars: The Frustrations of Over-Explaining

Mansplaining and Womensplaining can both lead to resentment and frustration. It's like being stuck in a cave without fire during a snowstorm — you're cold, irritated, and wondering why your partner can't just appreciate your knowledge of fire-making without trying to reinvent the wheel or the fire pit. Instead of feeling valued for your expertise, you feel undermined and dismissed, as if your partner believes their way is superior despite your proven experience. This dynamic can create a chilly atmosphere in the relationship, where instead of collaboration and mutual respect, there's a constant undercurrent of competition and condescension.

Over time, this can erode the foundation of trust and equality, making it difficult for partners to communicate openly and effectively. The one being explained to might start to feel belittled and undervalued, leading to growing resentment. Meanwhile, the one doing the explaining may become frustrated by what they perceive as the other's lack of appreciation or understanding. This vicious cycle of over-explaining and under-appreciation can transform simple conversations into battlegrounds, where the goal is no longer to share knowledge but to assert dominance.

Breaking free from this cycle requires both partners to recognize the impact of their actions and actively foster an environment of mutual respect. By valuing each other's knowledge and contributions, partners can create a warmer, more cooperative atmosphere—like a cozy cave where everyone's fire-making skills are acknowledged and appreciated without the need for over-the-top demonstrations. Imagine a world where cavepeople swap tips on mammoth hunting and berry gathering without anyone feeling like they're attending a prehistoric TED Talk. Embrace the idea that everyone's inner caveman and cavewoman have something valuable to share, and you'll be rocking the cave life together in no time!

By assuming someone needs information explained solely based on their gender, over explaining can overlook the other person's expertise or perspective. It's like missing out on discovering a revolutionary new way to sharpen flint because you're too busy giving a basic tool-making lecture to someone who already has their own secret flint-sharpening hack.

Picture trying to teach a mammoth how to dance when it already knows all the best moves—you end up missing out on an epic mammoth dance-off!

Equality Undermined: The Hidden Cost of Over-explaining

Engaging in over-explaining can undermine efforts toward gender equality and mutual respect. It perpetuates a dynamic where one gender assumes superiority in knowledge or understanding over the other, rather than fostering equal participation and respect in conversations. It's like stepping back from a collaborative hunt to argue about who's better at tracking without realizing that both skills are crucial for catching dinner.

When one partner repeatedly takes on the role of the explainer, it can create an imbalance in the relationship. This behavior suggests that one person's insights and understanding are more valuable, thereby diminishing the contributions of the other. This not only affects the immediate conversation but also sets a precedent for future interactions, reinforcing a pattern where one partner's voice dominates.

This imbalance can have long-term effects on the relationship. The person on the receiving end of over-explaining might begin to feel less confident in their abilities and knowledge, leading to a decreased willingness to participate in discussions or share their viewpoints. Over time, this can erode self-esteem and create a sense of inequality that permeates other aspects of the relationship.

Moreover, over-explaining can stifle the development of mutual respect and appreciation for each other's strengths. Instead of recognizing and valuing each other's unique skills and perspectives, partners may fall into a pattern of undervaluing the contributions of the other. This can prevent the relationship from growing into a true partnership based on equality and shared respect.

Moreover, over-explaining can hinder the development of mutual respect and appreciation for each other's strengths. Instead of recognizing and valuing each other's unique skills and perspectives, partners may undervalue one another's contributions. This dynamic can prevent the relationship from evolving into a true partnership based on equality and shared respect.

For gender equality to truly thrive, both partners must actively engage in and value each other's contributions. This involves recognizing when explaining becomes condescending and making a conscious effort to listen and respect each other's knowledge. Encouraging open dialogue and equal participation can help dismantle the dynamics that lead to over-ex plaining, fostering a healthier, more balanced relationship.

By being aware of these dynamics and striving for genuine equality in communication, partners can ensure their relationship is built on mutual respect and collaboration. This not only strengthens their bond but also sets a positive example for practicing equality in everyday interactions.

Tackling over-explaining involves navigating the rocky terrain of communication where cavewomen convey their knowledge of gathering berries or crafting the best loincloths without making the caveman feel like he's being lectured on how to sharpen his spear. It's about finding a balance where both can swap tips on mammoth hunting and cave painting without triggering arguments over who knows more about cave safety. Imagine discussing cave decor without one partner turning into the resident cave professor. This approach fosters a supportive and equitable environment where everyone's inner caveman and cavewoman feel valued and respected, keeping the peace in the cave and ensuring no one ends up sleeping next to the mammoth dung.

Mansplaining and womensplaining often emerge in discussions about the best way to build a sturdy fire or organize cave decorations. It's like when one caveperson insists on explaining the finer points of taming a wild boar while the other tries to teach how to weave intricate patterns into their animal skins. These dynamics highlight how misunderstandings can arise when one assumes their partner needs a lesson on spear-throwing instead of appreciating their expertise in choosing the right berries for dinner. Ultimately, both mansplaining and womensplaining can turn a cozy cave conversation into a battle over who gets to decide where to hang the latest cave paintings or whether to use firewood or dried leaves for the evening fire.

Ultimately, effective communication between cavemen and cavewomen is essential for building strong, harmonious relationships. The humorous but insightful examples of miscommunication highlight the need for both sides to understand and adapt to each other's unique conversational styles. Cavemen often approach conversations with a focus on facts and straightforward responses, while cavewomen typically seek empathy and connection. Recognizing these differences can help bridge the gap and reduce misunderstandings. By actively listening, valuing each other's perspectives, and avoiding assumptions based on gender, couples can foster a more supportive and equitable dynamic. Ultimately, navigating the complexities of caveman chat skills is about embracing each other's communication strengths, creating a more balanced and enjoyable relationship for both partners. From grunts to greatness, the journey of improving communication is a testament to the enduring human quest for connection and understanding.

Chapter 13

Mammoth Miscommunications: Talk Like a Caveman

Cavemen and Cavewomen manage communication like trying to start a fire without flint—completely different and occasionally explosive. When Cavewomen feel overwhelmed, they're like a volcanic eruption of emotions, while Cavemen turn into silent monks pondering life's mysteries (like why mammoths won't just fall into their traps). Cavewomen find solace in discussing their feelings, but Cavemen prefer tackling problems with all the emotional finesse of a mammoth charging into battle. If they don't understand each other's methods, it's like trying to start a fire by rubbing sticks and stones together—friction all around!

Imagine the scene: Caveman's on his mobile, silently scrolling through mammoth memes in his cave bathroom sanctuary (a sacred place for deep thoughts and online hunting tips), while Cavewoman is venting about the latest saber-toothed tiger encounter. Caveman's thinking, "Why can't she solve this like I do, with a spear and some luck?" Meanwhile, Cavewoman wonders why Caveman won't engage in her emotional mammoth hunt. It's like they're speaking different prehistoric languages—Caveman in grunts and nods, Cavewoman in detailed tales of the hunt.

To bridge these communication gaps, Cavemen and Cavewomen need a prehistoric Rosetta Stone—a guide to decode each other's cave paintings and grunts. When Caveman retreats into his silent cave, he's not ignoring Cavewoman; he's solving the puzzle of why the mammoth traps keep failing. Once he emerges with a solution (or a fresh mammoth meme), he's ready to engage. Understanding these quirks can turn cave conflicts into cooperative mammoth hunts—where both Caveman and Cavewoman bring their unique skills to the cave-dwelling table.

Caveman Throwing a Tantrum: The Prehistoric Rant!

Caveman's primal grumblings echo through the cave like a thunderstorm in a teapot. "Ugh, Oof, Grrrrr, ug!" he bellows, venting his frustration with the subtlety of a stampeding mammoth. Meanwhile, from the depths of the cave, Cavewoman deciphers his guttural language and promptly intervenes: "Eek, me cavewoman come to speak: grug!"

Caveman Translation

I sense there's a problem, and I need to fix it ASAP before my partner swoops in with her expert guidance and endless suggestions!

If a caveman can't find a solution to his woes, he dives headfirst into distraction mode. You'll catch him glued to the cave's version of the "news scrolls," hoping to lose himself in the latest saber-toothed tiger sightings or volcanic eruptions. If that's not cutting it, he'll upgrade to level two: epic battles of rock-paper-spear on his cave console, because nothing beats digital mammoth hunting to clear the mind.

When stress hits peak volcanic eruption levels, he might even go all out with extreme sports—like watching the Wheel of Fire race or the epic Boulder Toss Championships—anything to divert his attention from that nagging existential mammoth in the room.

Meanwhile, men have perfected the art of problem-solving in solitary confinement, deep in the back caves of their minds. It's their man-cave sanctuary, where the echoes of grunts and the flickering of cave torches provide the ideal ambiance for wrestling with life's mysteries.

Why do men prefer the cave hermit life? Blame it on ancient societal norms and gender stereotypes that dictate real men must conquer challenges with the grace of a charging woolly rhino and the silence of a nocturnal prowler. From an early age, they're taught that revealing their emotional struggles is like offering up their last mammoth steak to a roaming saber-toothed tiger—dangerous and unwise.

Next time you stumble upon a caveman lost in the depths of his cave or intensely scrutinizing a rock formation, spare a thought for his noble quest: the eternal battle against everyday mammoths, and the elusive quest for peace, quiet, and the occasional cave snack. Cavemen may be less inclined to openly discuss their problems with other cavemen due to several reasons deeply rooted in societal expectations and gender norms:

Socialization

Socialization starts early for cavemen—picture them at the tender age of five, solemnly swearing allegiance to the ancient code of "Don't Cry, Or Else the Cave Lions Will Get You." From that moment on, vulnerability becomes as elusive as a dodo bird at a Pterodactyl Convention.

Fear of Judgment

Fear of Judgment lurks around every corner of the cave. Cavemen would rather wrestle a saber-toothed tiger with their bare hands than risk a raised eyebrow from their fellow hunters for admitting they're having a bad mammoth-hunting day. Stoic is the name of the game—tears are as rare as a sunny day in the Ice Age.

Stigma Around Emotional Expression

Emotional Expression? More like Emotional Suppression. It's not just frowned upon—it's like trying to start a campfire with wet wood. The unspoken rule: emotions are for the woolly mammoths to stomp on, not for sharing over a roasted lizard with the tribe.

Cultural Norms

Cultural Norms are etched in stone tablets (metaphorically speaking, of course). Traditional masculinity demands independence, toughness, and emotional resilience—basically, being able to wrestle a woolly rhino while reciting epic tales of cave conquests without breaking a sweat.

Lack of Role Models

As for Role Models, forget about finding a caveman philosopher waxing poetic about his feelings by the campfire. The few who dare to mention they're having a rough day are swiftly branded as outliers—like the caveman who tried to invent the wheel before realizing round things roll downhill faster than you can say "mammoth stampede."

It's worth noting that these are generalizations—like trying to generalize the odds of encountering a saber-toothed tiger during a morning stroll. Many cavemen do indeed seek support and discuss their mammoth-sized problems with close friends or family members. As societal attitudes evolve and awareness spreads about mental health and emotional well-being, more cavemen might even consider sharing their struggles instead of trying to wrestle a mammoth alone in their mental cave gym.

Meanwhile, the caveman feels like a conqueror of the cave when he independently solves his issues in his private space (i.e., cave). It's his sacred man cave where he grunts, ponders, and occasionally figures out how to finally get the stone wheel to roll smoothly. Victory is sweet when it's just him and the satisfaction of a problem solved—no need for applause or a saber-toothed pat on the back.

Cavewoman's Approach: Sharing and Caring

As for Cavewomen, they navigate the treacherous terrain of daily life by seeking out trusted fellow cavewomen. When a Cavewoman feels overwhelmed, confused, or just plain dino-dung-tired, she doesn't hesitate to share with her tribe of sisters. It's not just venting; it's a sacred ritual of love and trust among cavewomen—like sharing the secret of where to find the ripest berries or how to tame a stubborn cave bear.

For Cavewomen, admitting to having problems is about as normal as finding a good spot to gather nuts. They don't derive self-worth from appearing mammoth-tamingly competent but from nurturing loving relationships and knowing they can unleash their inner cave-roar when needed. Whether it's feelings of being overwhelmed, confused, or just tired of picking twigs out of their hair, Cavewomen find fulfillment in sharing their ups and downs with their cave sisters. It's not just problem-solving; it's cavewoman camaraderie at its finest. Women often seek out other women they trust looking for:

Empathy

Women often believe that other women can better understand their experiences and emotions because they've collectively battled through more struggles than Grog did when he invented the wheel. Shared societal and gender-related challenges create bonds tighter than a mammoth's grip on the last patch of grass. It's like they have a secret club where the password is "Been there, survived that."

Emotional Support

Women are masters at navigating the treacherous waters of emotional connections. They seek out fellow women who can provide empathy, validation, and comfort during difficult times—like when the tribe runs out of berries and Atouk forgets their cave-anniversary. Nothing says solidarity like a group of women consoling each other over Atouk latest blunder, armed with berry wine and empathetic hugs.

Shared Experiences

Women have a knack for finding common ground quicker than Grog can start a fire with two rocks. Whether it's tackling gender roles, navigating family dynamics, or dodging societal expectations like dodging a charging woolly rhino, shared experiences forge bonds stronger than a cave bear's handshake. They might even have a secret handshake—though it's more likely to involve comforting pats on the back and shared sighs of exasperation.

Communication Styles

When it comes to discussing personal matters, women have their own secret language that even Grog can't decipher. They feel more comfortable with fellow women who speak the language of listening, empathy, and emotional expression—because sometimes, a grunt just won't cut it. Imagine Grog trying to join the conversation with his well-meaning but utterly misplaced grunts of support; it's a recipe for comedic disaster.

Trust and Confidentiality: Keeping Secrets Tighter Than Grog's Stone Club

Women value trust and confidentiality as highly as Grog treasures his prized stone club. They confide in other women they trust to keep secrets more securely than a saber-toothed tiger guards its den. Safe spaces and reliable confidantes ensure that women can express their thoughts and feelings without fear of those secrets becoming gossip around the tribal fire. After all, no one wants their deepest secrets turning into Grog's latest campfire tale.

Seeking support from other women is like discovering a stash of perfectly ripe berries after a long day of mammoth hunting—refreshing, satisfying, and always shared with those who understand that sometimes, the biggest challenge is keeping Grog from eating them all at once!

The Ancient Art of Gentle Reminders

Nagging: the ancient art of repeatedly reminding your caveman to do something until he caves in and does it just to make you stop. It's like playing hide and seek with a woolly mammoth—no matter how hard you try to hide from it, it always finds you!

Remember, a caveman hides in the bathroom to escape from the family because it's the only place where he can grunt in peace and pretend he's hunting mammoths instead of tackling the endless list of cave chores. It's like trying to tame a wild beast—except in this case, the beast is just a caveman who can't seem to remember where the trash can is! Here are a few potential reasons why someone might nag:

Communication Styles: Repeating the Obvious Until Grog Gets It

The subtle art of saying the same thing over and over until your caveman finally caves in. It's like trying to teach a pet dinosaur a new trick—except the trick is remembering to take out the trash! You find yourself repeating, "Can you please take out the trash?" until Grog looks up from his rock collection with a confused grunt. It's a delicate dance of persistence and patience, much like trying to get a dinosaur to roll over.

Expectations: The Great Mammoth Hunt of Household Chores

Nagging often arises when there's a gap between what your cavewoman expects and what actually happens. It's like expecting your spear to hit the mammoth on the first throw, but it keeps missing, and you have to keep trying until you finally get dinner! You expect Grog to remember to clean up, but it's more like watching him aimlessly wander the cave, missing the target entirely. Persistence pays off eventually, right?

Frustration: Fire Starting in the Rain

Nagging can also be a way to release pent-up frustration in a relationship. It's like trying to light a fire in the rain—sometimes you just need to keep striking that flint until you get a spark! Each reminder about chores or responsibilities is another strike of the flint, hoping for that magical moment when Grog actually lights up and gets things done. Meanwhile, you're left wondering if it'll ever stop raining in your cave.

Cultural and Social Norms: The Cavewoman's Guide to Task Management

In many caves, there's an unspoken rule that women manage the tasks and emotional labor. So when things aren't done, nagging becomes a reminder of who's really in charge—the one who knows where everything is stored! While Grog is busy inventing new tools or bragging about his latest rock discovery, you're managing the cave inventory and making sure everyone's fed. It's a constant juggling act, ensuring the cave doesn't fall into chaos.

Perceived Importance: It's Not Just a Rock, It's a Big Deal

Sometimes what seems like nagging to one person is just a cavewoman's way of saying, "I care about this as much as you care about that new rock you found." It's not about the message; it's about the deep emotional attachment to getting things done right the first time! To you, making sure the cave is clean and organized is as important as Grog's prized rock collection. And if he could understand that, life in the cave would be a lot smoother.

Addressing nagging in a relationship is like navigating a labyrinth with only a torch made of patience and a map of emotional landmines. It's all about decoding the hidden messages behind "Did you take out the trash?" and "Could you please put the seat down?"

While men often see nagging as a tactical maneuver for their partner to steer them toward doing what needs to be done (or what she wants), deep down, it's a gentle reminder of her undying affection—albeit delivered with the subtlety of a mammoth stampede.

Male Nagging: The Gentle Art of Man-Pestering

Male nagging, or as some cavewomen affectionately call it, "man-pestering," "prodding," or simply "nagging," involves a nuanced dance of persistence and obliviousness that can rival even the most skilled hunter's tracking abilities. It's not just about reminding her to put the mammoth hide back in the cave; it's an art form.

While women might nudge their partners about taking out the trash or fixing the roof, men might gently prod about everything from needing more alone time to "subtly" suggesting a romantic evening (hint: it usually involves fire and meat). It's all in good intentions, of course, even if it comes across as about as subtle as a saber-toothed tiger in a tea shop.

Nagging Might Be Seen As:

Repetitive Requests from Cavewomen "Honey, did you remember to sharpen the spear?"

Five minutes later "Did you sharpen the spear yet?"

Repetitive Requests for Zug Zug from Cavemen "Hey babe, it's been a while since we..."

Five minutes later "What about now?"

Five more minutes later "How about now?"

Five + five more minutes later "Are you sure now isn't a good time?"

Monitoring or Checking-In "Just making sure you're feeding the fire properly. Can't have it going out, you know?"

Setting Ultimatums or Demands "If we don't organize the cave by sunset, there will be no mammoth stew for a week!"

Focused Criticism "Do you really need to bring in that many rocks? It's cluttering up the cave."

Control or Micromanagement "I'll take care of the hunting plans, the fire-building, and the cave organization. Just sit back and relax."

It's all in the quest for cave harmony, even if it sometimes feels like navigating through a woolly mammoth stampede. Balancing expectations and chores is just part of maintaining peace in the prehistoric household.

Ultimately, both men and women can have their moments of "nagging" in relationships, whether it's about chores, communication, or even the frequency of intimacy. It's like trying to navigate a mammoth-sized debate club in the cave. The key is for both partners to keep their stone tools sharp—communication-wise—and to listen to each other without turning every conversation into a prehistoric battle of wills.

Chapter 14

Gender Roles: From Mammoths to Modernity

In ancient times, cavemen hunted mammoths and expected their cavewomen to turn the catch into a gourmet meal. Meanwhile, cavewomen gathered berries and relied on their cavemen to fend off saber-toothed tigers and, of course, spiders. This dynamic continues today, albeit with fewer tigers and more grocery runs.

Marriage, an ancient social contract, is like signing up for a lifelong membership at the "Dinosaurs Anonymous" club. It's where two people promise to stick together through thick and thin, for better or worse, and not kill each other over whose turn it is to take out the trash. Plus, it's not just about having babies; it's about trading resources, like who gets the last slice of pizza and who picks the Netflix show.

Whether trading mammoth tusks or binge-watching TV series, marriage is a partnership that brings families together. It's like ancient bartering, but instead of haggling over rocks and bones, you're negotiating whose turn it is to walk the woolly mammoth (also known as the dog).

Ever notice how your friend ends up dating a caveman who's more trouble than a mammoth on a rampage? Despite all the warning grunts, there's something oddly irresistible about these guys with a rebellious streak. Maybe it's the way they swing their club or the way they roar instead of talk.

Why are these wild men so appealing, even when we know they might leave us with more emotional bruises than a run-in with a saber-toothed tiger? It's like they've got this primal charm that's impossible to resist like they've unlocked the secret to seduction without even trying. We asked the experts, but all they could say was, "Well, he's got that caveman confidence, you know? And that's hot."

Cavewomen just can't resist a guy who's more trouble than a pterodactyl in a pottery shop. It's like they're magnetic – they draw you in with their raw, untamed energy, and you end up wondering if you should have stuck with the nice caveman who knows how to start a fire without burning down the whole cave.

"He's like a chocolate cake - I know he's bad for me, but I can't resist... especially when he's got that caveman charm that's more tempting than a fresh kill."

Evolutionary biologists describe 'bad boys' as hypermasculine, like cavemen. They project strength and an alpha male presence, often showing rebelliousness and emotional distance. In extreme cases, these men may show traits like narcissism, antisocial behavior, and impulsiveness. Yet, despite these negative traits, women are drawn to them due to our cavewoman genetics.

"Dating a caveman is like riding a roller coaster without a safety harness - exhilarating and terrifying at the same time. It's like a cavewoman's brain is screaming, 'Run!' while simultaneously thinking, 'But what a ride!'"

Part of the attraction to bad boys can be explained by evolutionary biology. Some women are more attracted to masculine men, like strong cavemen, especially when younger and more fertile. These men may have better genes, which unconsciously appeal to women at an evolutionary level. Women often mention traits like integrity and respectfulness when asked about their ideal partner. They actively avoid partners who are rude or aggressive, knowing that bad boys aren't suitable for long-term relationships.

"I know I should stay away, but his bad boy charm is like a magnet pulling me in. It's like my evolutionary wiring is saying, 'Go for the guy who can wrestle a mammoth,' even though I know I should be looking for the one who can make a decent fire and cuddle after."

Young cavewomen are naturally rebellious and often attracted to rebellious cavemen. These traits are usually suppressed during childhood when girls are taught to conform. If a cavewoman's inner life isn't expressed, she might be drawn to a bad boy to live out her rebellion through him. Humans are often attracted to qualities in others that they wish they had; she admires his freedom. Despite this, which makes cavemen unsuitable for long-term partners, it can make them very attractive and worth the risk of heartache.

"Dating him is like playing with fire, and I've never been more willing to get burned. It's like my cavewoman brain is saying, 'Let's see how close we can get to that roaring flame without getting singed."

Especially when women are bored, these cavemen seem exciting, adventurous, and a change from the norm. However, dating such a bad boy can bring emotional pain, conflict, and heartache. Bad boys have a taboo allure, strengthening desire even when we know it's not best for long-term stability.

"They say nice guys finish last, but I never expected to end up in a drag race. I guess cavewomen like a little speed and danger now and then!"

True cavemen aren't quick to commit to one partner; they often have many relationships before settling down. Cavewomen feel accomplished if they can get a true caveman to commit to a monogamous relationship. They feel attractive, funny, and smart enough to win such a prize. Societal pressures often drive women to seek validation and feel 'enough.' Falling for these cavemen usually happens to caring and nurturing individuals who see the best in others and struggle to accept someone could be a 'bad boy' or a true caveman.

"It's like convincing a caveman to give up mammoth hunting for a steady supply of berries and nuts. You've gotta feel like you've really made an impression!"

Cavewomen who manage to bag a true caveman for a committed relationship are like the MVPs of the prehistoric dating scene. It's not just about winning his heart; it's about showing off your survival skills!

The Attraction Chronicles: Caveman Meets Cavewoman

Attraction is like trying to solve a Rubik's cube while it's on fire—confusing, frustrating, and sometimes you end up just throwing it out the window. Scientists are still unraveling the mysteries of attraction, like what happens in the brain when someone sees someone else as beautiful. It's like they're peeking into a caveman's brain to figure out why he suddenly decides mammoths are out and berries are in. On one side, there's the biological stuff—like testosterone making you crave feminine faces. On the other side, there's the social stuff—like trying to impress her with your fire-making skills while she's unimpressed by your caveman jokes.

I used to think I was a good listener until I dated a woman who remembers everything I say. Now I just nod and smile and hope she forgets how I burned dinner last week. When we delve into the biological side of attraction, remember: Cavemen and Cavewomen are animals by nature. Love and attraction are primal behaviors meant to help us mate, driven more by instincts than logic. It's like our brains are wired to chase after mates without a moment's thought—kind of like how I chase after that last piece of mammoth meat! Love, scientifically speaking, is just a bunch of chemicals in our bodies playing Cupid. Researchers are out there trying to crack the code of these hormones, these sneaky little messengers that make us feel all hot and bothered. So, figuring out these chemicals is like solving a puzzle that might lead to the secrets of attraction—though, honestly, it sometimes feels more like deciphering a mystery novel.

"She's like a mystery novel – intriguing, unpredictable, and I have no idea what's going to happen next."

Lust, Attraction, and Attachment: The Cave Person's Guide to Prehistoric Love

It's like a caveman's trilogy of love, but with less drama and more grunting. See, for us Cavemen, it's all about physical attraction—like when you see a well-cooked mammoth leg and can't resist taking a big bite. Lust kicks in when you just want to be close, really close, to someone, enjoying that physical intimacy. And hey, it's not just about grunting and flexing; there are actual hormones at play here. Testosterone and estrogen are like the love potion of our time—making us feel all tingly and eager. They're the real MVPs when it comes to sparking that desire, bringing Cavemen and Cavewomen closer together, one primal urge at a time. Next time you're feeling that animal magnetism, thank your hormones—they're doing all the heavy lifting!"

"Lust is like a microwave – it heats things up fast, but it can also leave you burnt."

Attraction is like discovering fire for the first time—your brain's all like, 'Whoa, dopamine rush!' It's like winning a mammoth hunt and scoring the juiciest cut of meat. See, when you're attracted to someone, your brain's dishing out dopamine like it's the ultimate reward. It's that warm, fuzzy feeling that makes you want to stick around and hunt together forever. So yeah, it's more than just wanting to be close physically; it's about bonding on a deep, primal level. Your brain's reward system knows what's up—keeping you hooked on that sweet, sweet attraction, one dopamine hit at a time!

"Attachment is like WiFi – sometimes it's strong, sometimes it's weak, and you're never quite sure if it's going to drop."

Attachment is like finding the perfect cave to cozy up in after a mammoth hunt—safe, secure, and totally oxytocin-inducing! When the Caveman flexes his emotional muscles and pays attention to his Cavewoman, bam! Oxytocin floods the cave like a warm fire pit. It's that magical hormone that says, 'Hey, I'm feeling all warm and fuzzy inside because you're here.' It's like wrapping yourself in a mammoth fur blanket after a long day of hunting—comforting, reassuring, and love-inducing. And get this, it doesn't just happen in romantic relationships; even friends can get cozy in their oxytocin caves, minus the lust and attraction drama. Regardless of whether it's love or friendship, oxytocin's got your back—keeping bonds tight and hearts warm!

"Attachment is like a Netflix series – you binge-watch it, get emotionally invested, and then wonder what to do when it's over."

Human relationships are like choosing the ripest fruit—there's the initial desire for the juiciest one (lust), but then there's that deeper, 'hey, you're actually really sweet inside' feeling (attraction). Looks matter, of course. When guys size up potential mates, beauty is often on the checklist. But just because a cavewoman's got cheekbones for days doesn't mean every caveman's swooning.

People usually pair up with someone about as appealing as they are themselves. Yet, we can't deny it—both men and women tend to gravitate toward partners they think are more eye-catching. It's like evolutionary Instagram out there, with everyone trying to swipe right on the hottest cave dwellers!

Understanding attraction is like trying to solve a puzzle blindfolded— you think you've got the pieces, but then someone flips the board and starts rearranging them. Personality adds a whole new layer of complexity. Sure, someone might be drop-dead gorgeous, but if their personality is more like a cave bear than a charming caveman, you'll quickly find yourself thinking, "No matter how good-looking they are, there's gotta be someone tired of their antics!" It's the halo effect in action—you might forgive a lot when someone's a total hottie, even if they're about as charming as a grumpy mammoth in mating season. Figuring out attractions? It's like navigating a maze blindfolded, with a distracting, handsome Minotaur at every turn.

"Attraction to a crazy woman is like being in a romantic comedy directed by Quentin Tarantino – unexpected plot twists and lots of adrenaline."

While the halo effect might convince you that someone's honesty shines brighter just because they look good, it's a slippery slope. Sure, cavemen want someone they can trust, but if you've got a dishonest charmer on your hands, they might end up looking more like a sneaky cave weasel than a reliable partner. Studies say honesty is sexy—nothing like knowing your mate won't steal your last mammoth leg. But if you catch them fibbing, suddenly they're less attractive than a cave full of soggy fur blankets. It's like the halo effect put on its X-ray vision glasses—what looked like a perfect specimen turns out to be a hairy situation.

"Lust with a crazy woman is like trying to juggle flaming torches – it's impressive if you can pull it off, but it's bound to get messy."

Understanding attraction is like trying to bake a perfect mammoth pie—it's all about getting the right mix of looks and personality. Sure, there are some ingredients that most cavemen and cavewomen find tasty, like strong jawlines or a sense of humor sharper than a flint knife. But everyone's palate is different. Some cavewomen might go gaga for a guy who can start a fire with two sticks, while others prefer a caveman who can paint a mammoth on the cave wall like it's no big deal.

It's like being at a prehistoric buffet—you're scanning the crowd for that one dish that makes your tummy do the mammoth dance. And just when you think you've figured it out, someone throws in a surprise ingredient like kindness or a knack for storytelling that turns your attraction recipe upside down. While there are some universal flavors of attraction, at the end of the day, it's all about finding that special blend that makes your heart go thump-thump like a mammoth drum solo.

In conclusion, the evolution of gender roles from the days of hunting mammoths to modern times reflects a journey of adaptation, partnership, and shared responsibilities. Ancient cavemen and cavewomen worked together to survive, with each playing crucial roles in the hunt and home. Today, while the specifics have changed, the essence of partnership remains. Marriage continues to be a dynamic exchange, balancing love, support, and mutual respect. Though our tools and challenges have evolved, the foundational principles of cooperation and understanding between genders persist. By appreciating both historical context and contemporary dynamics, we can navigate relationships with a blend of tradition and modernity, ensuring that the spirit of collaboration and mutual care endures through the ages.

Chapter 15

Grunts to Conversations: Relationship Secrets Unlocked

Now that you've mastered the art of caveman communication, you're ready to navigate the rocky terrain of love like a pro. It's like leveling up from chiseling stone tools to crafting masterpieces—except your masterpiece now is a happy relationship, not a stone spear.

I've seen couples transform faster than a saber-tooth tiger spotting dinner, from awkward cave-side grunts to sharing mammoth steaks and laughter under the starry sky. You too can be that couple. Remember, men and women might as well be speaking different prehistoric languages sometimes, but with the right tools (and maybe a bit of cave art to illustrate your points), you'll be communicating like Neanderthal Shakespeare in no time. Sharpen those communication skills and get ready to conquer the wild world of relationships—it's a jungle out there, but with a little effort, you'll be swinging from vine to vine like Tarzan and Jane, minus the loincloth.

"A happy wife means a happy life and fewer 'honey-do' lists... and maybe even an occasional day off from couch assembly duty!"

But remember, love is like the seasons. Spring is all sunshine and flowers, but summer? That's when you realize maintaining a relationship is like trying to keep a campfire going in a rainstorm—hard work! Fall rolls around, and you're harvesting the fruits of your labor, but winter? That's when you're staring into the abyss, wondering why you ever thought sharing a cave was a good idea.

It's easy to forget all those relationship tips you learned when the going gets tough. Suddenly, you're grumbling about your partner hogging the fur blanket and forgetting to see things from their perspective. Remember, in the game of love, there's no off-season—keep your firewood dry and your cave warm, and you might just survive until spring!

"I love you, but if you touch the thermostat one more time, I'm booking us a one-way trip to Antarctica!"

When you feel emotionally empty, like in 'winter,' you might feel sad and question yourself and your relationship. It's okay to feel unsure or upset but remember, it's all part of how love goes. Things often seem darkest just before they start to get better.

"Yes, I know I'm a man, but even I need directions sometimes. Especially when assembling furniture or navigating the mall during the holiday shopping season!"

To do well in relationships, we must understand and accept these different phases of love. Sometimes, love is easy, like remembering where you left your keys. Other times, it takes work, like trying to fold a fitted sheet. We can't always expect our partners—or ourselves—to show love perfectly all the time. It's important to be kind to ourselves and not expect to remember everything we've learned about loving and caring for each other. After all, even Google Maps reroutes sometimes!

"Why do you only hear what you want to hear? It's like having selective hearing but with a PhD in filtering out the stuff you don't want to deal with."

Learning means hearing things over and over again until they finally stick. It's like trying to remember your WiFi password—you hear it a hundred times, forget it, curse a bit, and then suddenly it pops back into your head at the most random moment. So, if you're feeling a bit lost or confused, just remember that relationships are like navigating with a GPS in a foreign country—sometimes you'll take the wrong turn, but eventually, you'll figure out where you're going.

Ultimately, understanding that men and women think differently isn't like discovering a secret cheat code for relationship success. It's also not about knowing everything perfectly; it's about using this wisdom to navigate the maze of love without getting stuck in the wrong corner. Let's keep communicating, discussing, and not judging—unless it's about your sock collection. Here's to more love and less laundry! Cheers to your journey ahead!

"Marriage is like cave painting: the caveman tries to hunt mammoths while the cavewoman decorates the cave!"

Chapter 16

Love Through the Ages: From Fire to Tinder

In today's dating world, swiping on Tinder parallels the ancient practices of Caveman and Cavewoman, highlighting our timeless quest for companionship amidst modern complexities. Dating today is deeply rooted in primal instincts and the essential human need for friendship and intimacy, echoing back to the days of our prehistoric ancestors. Despite evolving methods and societal norms, the fundamental motivations for seeking romantic connections have endured across human history. Cavemen would say, "Marriage is like a deck of cards. In the beginning, all you need are two hearts and a diamond. By the end, you wish you had a club and a spade."

This book delved into these enduring aspects of human nature, exploring their relevance across diverse relationship dynamics, including LGBTQ+ partnerships. It examined the intricate interplay of biological, psychological, and social factors shaping attraction and connection in contemporary relationships. Reflecting on personal experiences within my own familial and social circles, I've grown to appreciate the complexities individuals navigate in forming and sustaining relationships.

Observing our children as they navigate friendships in school and beyond has illuminated the challenges young people encounter in understanding themselves and their peers amidst the complexities of adolescence. Similarly, witnessing my wife's journey through university and beyond has offered insights into the distinct realm of female dynamics—its intricacies, obstacles, and rewards—distinct from those encountered by men.

In the curious realm of relationships and the wild world of dating, figuring out the dynamics can feel like deciphering hieroglyphics after a few too many fermented berries. It's a mix of biological urges, psychological needs, and social pressures that turn dates into a prehistoric soap opera. Understanding these dynamics is crucial—after all, you don't want to bring a saber-toothed tiger to the mammoth hunt of love!

From the Stone Age to the swipe-right age, dating has evolved like a slow-cooked mammoth stew—some parts ancient tradition, some parts futuristic tech, and a whole lot of awkward flirting in between. Whether you're carving love notes on cave walls or DMing emojis on your phone, the quest for companionship persists like an eternal hunt for the perfect mammoth. This book delved into these timeless quests, unpacking why we still chase after love despite having more distractions than a cave full of shiny rocks.

As I ponder the wild rollercoaster ride of dating and relationships, I can't help but think it's like trying to tame a woolly mammoth—exciting, terrifying, and occasionally covered in surprises. From playground crushes to adulting awkwardness, figuring out ourselves and each other is like deciphering ancient cave paintings—sometimes baffling, often enlightening, and usually involving a lot of grunts and gestures. And let's not forget navigating the roles of modern-day men and women; it's like trying to blend Stone Age instincts with smartphone etiquette—tricky, but occasionally surprisingly civilized.

Despite all the dating apps and modern complexities, one thing remains as timeless as a prehistoric rock: our unyielding quest for emotional fulfillment, companionship, and not having to eat mammoth meat alone.

By digging into the nuances of attraction and relationship dynamics, we can better understand why we swipe right (or left) and why we sometimes end up in situations that feel more like a cave painting gone wrong. Finally, as we stumble through modern dating, let's hold onto our primal instincts and remember that finding love is like discovering fire—sometimes you get burned, but sometimes it keeps you warm through those cold, lonely nights.

Caveman Chronicles: The Sources

Alexander, Gerianne M., and Barbara B. Sherwin. "Sex Differences in Patterns of Sexual Arousal: A Developmental Perspective." The Role of Theory in Sex Research, edited by John Bancroft, Indiana University Press, 1993, pp. 83-101.

Bancroft, J. (1988). Human sexuality and its problems. Churchill Livingstone.

Bancroft, J., & Wu, F. C. W. (1983). Changes in erectile responsiveness during androgen replacement therapy. Archives of Sexual Behavior, 12(1), 59-66. https://doi.org/10.1007/BF01542004

Beck, Julie, Alice Bozman, and Timothy Qualtrough. "Sexual Desire Disorders: A Comparative Study of Gender Differences." Journal of Sex & Marital Therapy, vol. 17, no. 2, 1991, pp. 105-119. DOI: 10.1080/00926239108404341

Chapman, G. (1995). The five love languages: How to express heartfelt commitment to your mate. Northfield Publishing.

Chapman, G. (2015). The 5 love languages: The secret to love that lasts (Revised ed.). Northfield Publishing.

Chivers, M. L., Rieger, G., Latty, E., & Bailey, J. M. (2004). A sex difference in the specificity of sexual arousal. Psychological Science, 15(11), 736-744. https://doi.org/10.1111/j.0956-7976.2004.00750.x

Chivers, M. L., Seto, M. C., & Blanchard, R. (2007). Gender and sexual orientation differences in sexual response to sexual activities versus gender of actors in sexual films. Journal of Personality and Social Psychology, 93(6), 1108-1121. https://doi.org/10.1037/0022-3514.93.6.1108

Dabbs, J. M. (2000). Heroes, rogues, and lovers: Testosterone and behavior. McGraw-Hill.

Del Carlo, Lauren (2007) "Between the Sacred Mountains: A Cultural History of the Dineh," ESSAI: Vol. 5, Article 15. Available at: http://dc.cod.edu/essai/vol5/iss1/15

Eysenck, H. J. (1971). The psychology of sex. Penguin Books.

Gray, J. (1992). Men are from Mars, women are from Venus. HarperCollins.

Jones, W. H., & Barlow, D. H. (1990). Sexual dysfunction in men and women: Etiology, assessment, and treatment. Guilford Press.

Gottman, J. M., & DeClaire, J. (2001). The relationship cure: A 5 step guide to strengthening your marriage, family, and friendships. Harmony Books.

Gottman, J. M., & Silver, N. (1999). The seven principles for making marriage work. Harmony Books.

Hendrix, H., & Hunt, H. L. K. (1993). Keeping the love you find: A personal guide. Pocket Books.

Keesing, Roger M., and Felix M. Keesing. New Perspectives in Cultural Anthropology. Holt, Rinehart and Winston, 1971. ISBN 0-03-085486-5.

Kin Groups and Social Structure. Holt, Rinehart and Winston, 1975. Reprinted by Thomson Learning, 1985. ISBN 0-03-012846-3.

Kirshenbaum, M. (2000). The weekend marriage: Abundant love in a time-starved world. Harmony Books.

Laumann, E. O., Gagnon, J. H., Michael, R. T., & Michaels, S. (1994). The social organization of sexuality: Sexual practices in the United States. University of Chicago Press.

Leitenberg, H., & Henning, K. (1995). Sexual fantasy. Psychological Bulletin, 117(3), 469-496. https://doi.org/10.1037/0033-2909.117.3.469

Marks, M. & Fieds, B. (2005). Why do men have nipples? Hundreds of questions you'd only ask a doctor after your third martini. Three Rivers Press.

Mazur, A., & Booth, A. (1998). Testosterone and dominance in men. Behavioral and Brain Sciences, 21(3), 353-397. https://doi.org/10.1017/S0140525X98001228

Mean Girls. Directed by Mark Waters, performances by Lindsay Lohan, Rachel McAdams, and Tina Fey, Paramount Pictures, 2004.

Minocher, R., Thomas, M. L., & Laland, K. N. (2018). The evolution of cultural evolution. Evolution and Human Behavior, 39(6), 608-620. https://doi.org/10.1016/j.evolhumbehav.2018.11.003

Mitchell, Kirstin R., et al. "Why Do Men Report More Opposite-Sex Sexual Partners Than Women? Analysis of the Gender Discrepancy in a British National Probability Survey." The Journal of Sex Research, vol. 56, no. 1, 2019, pp. 1-8, doi:10.1080/00224499.2018.1481193. PMCID: PMC6326215. PMID: 30044926.

Nutter, A. W., & Condron, M. K. (1983). Understanding human sexuality. McGraw-Hill.

Prause, N., & Pfaus, J. G. (2015). Viewing sexual stimuli associated with greater sexual responsiveness, not erectile dysfunction. Sexual Medicine, 3(2), 90-98. https://doi.org/10.1002/sm2.58

Perel, E. (2006). Mating in captivity: Unlocking erotic intelligence. HarperCollins.

Perel, E. (2017). The state of affairs: Rethinking infidelity. HarperCollins.

Prause, N., Steele, V. R., Staley, C., Sabatinelli, D., & Hajcak, G. (2015). Modulation of late positive potentials by sexual images in problem users and controls inconsistent with "porn addiction". Biological Psychology, 109, 192-199. https://doi.org/10.1016/j.biopsycho.2015.06.005

Prause, N., & Janssen, E. (2006). Blood oxygenation level dependent response to sexual stimuli in women and men using continuous versus event-related designs. Journal of

Sexual Medicine, 3(3), 283-291. https://doi.org/10.1111/j.1743-6109.2006.00218.x

Quinn, Naomi. 1982. "'Commitment' in American Marriage: A Cultural Analysis." American Ethnologist 9 (4): 755-798.

Real, T. (2002). How can I get through to you? Reconnecting men and women. Scribner.

Real, T. (2007). The new rules of marriage: What you need to know to make love work. Ballantine Books.

Schreiner-Engel, P., Schiavi, R. C., Smith, H., & White, D. (1982). Sexual arousability and the menstrual cycle. Psychosomatic Medicine, 44(1), 67-76. https://doi.org/10.1097/00006842-198201000-00008

Schreiner-Engel, P. (1989). Sexual behavior: Problems and management. Guilford Press.

Sacks, H. (1992) Lectures on Conversation, Vol. I. Cambridge, MA: Blackwell.

Sanusi, A., 2022. 7 qualities that men look for in a woman. The Nigerian Tribune. December 13, 2022. https://tribuneonlineng.com/7-qualities-that-men-look-for-in-a-woman/#:~:text=Men%20love%20women%20who%20are,and%20warmth%20from%20her%20heart

Smithsonian National Museum of Natural History, 2024. Climate Effects on Human Evolution. Accessed March 20, 2024. https://humanorigins.si.edu/research/climate-and-human-evolutio/climate-effects-human-evolution

The Kinsey Institute. "The Kinsey Institute for Research in Sex, Gender, and Reproduction." The Kinsey Institute, https://kinseyinstitute.org/index.php. Accessed June 20, 2023

"What's Your Number?" Superdrug Online Doctor, https://onlinedoctor.superdrug.com/whats-your-number.html#:~:text=When%20it%20comes%20to%20 number,far%20off%20from%20the%20reality. Accessed July 14, 2023

Made in the USA
Middletown, DE
02 September 2024

60230184R00097